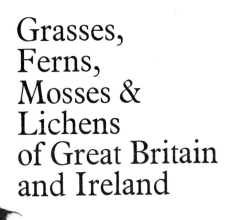

Grasses,
Ferns,
Mosses &
Lichens
of Great Britain
and Ireland

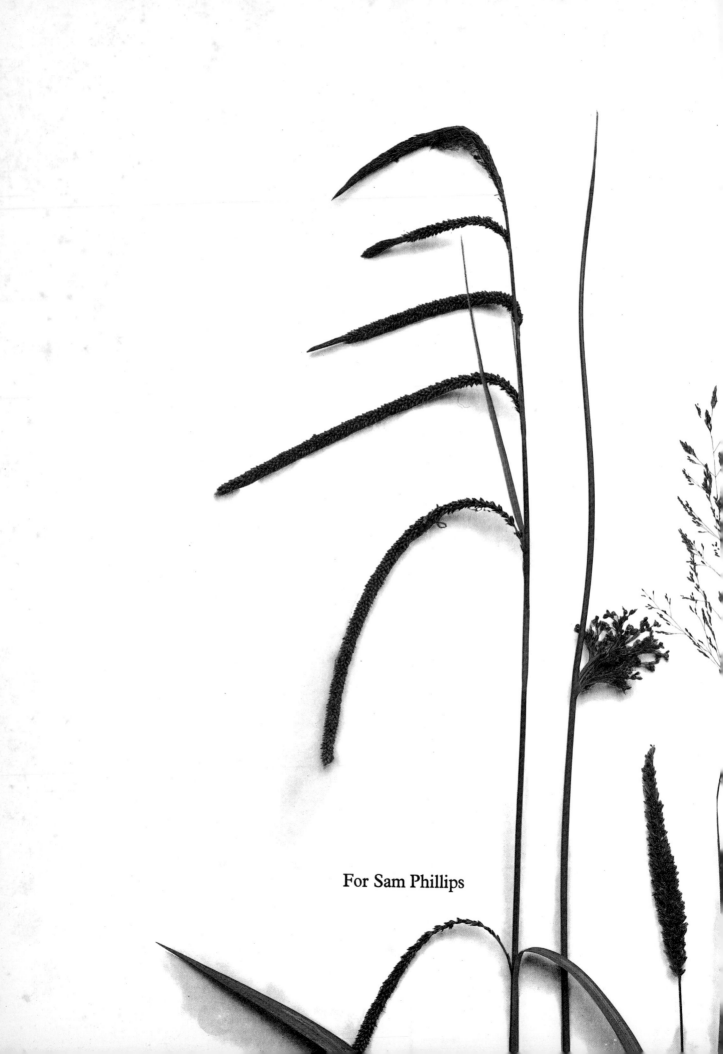

For Sam Phillips

Grasses, Ferns, Mosses & Lichens
of Great Britain and Ireland
by
Roger Phillips
assisted by Sheila Grant

Section Editors
Grasses: Martyn Rix
Ferns: Peter Barnes
Mosses: Alan Eddy
Lichens: J. R. Laundon

A Pan Original

Acknowledgements

A book like this is only possible with the help and cooperation of a great many people. At the Natural History Museum, A. I. Harrington gave a great deal of his time in checking the identification of mosses and liverworts, as did J. R. Laundon with the identification of the lichens. At Wisley, Martyn Rix checked the grasses, and Peter Barnes went through the ferns and their allies. In addition to this I would like to thank the following: David and Pat Batty, Pamela Bunting, Alan Christie, Beverly Clark, Alan Cook, Jenny Deakin, Duncan Donald, Nicky Foy, Elsie Grant, Brian Halliwell, Ray Hunter, John Mason, Kate Penoyre.

I am also grateful to the following organizations:

The British Museum (Natural History).
The Royal Botanic Gardens, Kew.
The Royal Horticultural Society, Wisley.
University of Cambridge Botanic Garden, Cambridge.
The National Trust at Ben Lawers.
The Nature Conservancy Council in Edinburgh and Huntingdon.

I would like to thank the following for allowing me to use their photographs:
Peter Barnes: 87(br), 98(br), 101(tr), 111(r), 114(l), 115(r). John Birks: 77(br), 81(br), 85(tr)(br), 102(br), 106(tr)(br), 107(tl), 115(tl)(bl), 120(tr)(bl), 122(br), 124(br), 126(tl)(tc)(bl)(bc), 128(bc), 129(tc), 134(bl), 137(tc)(bc), 138(tl)(tc)(tr)(br), 140(bl), 141(bl)(bc), 142(tl)(tc)(bl), 145(br), 148(tl)(bl), 149(tl), 150(tc)(tr), 157(br), 158(br), 163(tl)(tc)(tr)(br), 164(bl)(br), 168(bl), 169(tr), 173(tl), 174(br), 175(tl)(tc)(bc), 177(tl). Frances Davis: 170(tc). Peter James: 164(tc)(tr), 165(tl)(tc)(br), 168(tl), 171(tl)(bl), 174(bc), 177(bl), 180(tc), 184(bl), 185(tl), 187(tl). J. R. Laundon: 164(bc), 166(tr), 170(tl)(bl)(bc), 173(tr), 174(tc), 175(tr), 184(bl)(br). John Mason: 93(c), 107(c), 108(c). G. Matthews: 185(bc). Malcolm W. Storey: 119(bc), 120(tl)(br), 124(tc)(bc), 129(tl)(bc), 130(bl), 135(tl), 137(tl), 138(bl), 139(br), 141(tc), 142(tr), 144(bl), 154(br), 155(br), 159(br), 162(br), 163(bl)(bc), 165(bc), 166(tl)(tc)(bc), 174(bl), 176(tr), 177(tc), 178(tl), 180(tl), 183(tr), 185(tr)(bl), 187(br). Alan Outen: 107(bl), 119(tc)(tr), 120(bc), 124(tr), 125(bl), 127(bl), 129(bl), 138(bc), 141(tl), 150(bc)(br), 157(tr), 162(tl). (t-top, b-bottom, l-left, r-right, c-centre)

First published 1980 by Pan Books Ltd, Cavaye Place, London SW10 9PG
© Roger Phillips 1980
ISBN 0 330 25959 8

Printed in Great Britain by Cripplegate Printing Company Ltd, Edenbridge, Kent

Four colour origination by David Brin Limited, London EC1

Contents

Introduction

When I photographed *Wild Flowers of Britain*, I was unable to include the grasses, rushes and sedges, so I decided to tackle them together with a diverse selection of the less well known plants that may be found in Britain.

The point of the book is to provide an identification aid for those who like to work from illustrations rather than text and it is divided into four parts: firstly, grasses and their look-alikes; secondly, ferns and their allies; thirdly, mosses and liverworts; fourthly, lichens. The first two groups have a reasonably limited flora so I have been quite comprehensive; the second two groups, however, are very large and it is impossible to cover the whole subject, but at least I have been able to reproduce many more photographs than have been published previously.

How to use the book

The plants are divided into four main sections: grasses, ferns, mosses and lichens. Each section has been dealt with separately, with a specialist consultant editor verifying the material. Below are notes for each section explaining botanically how the ordering has been arrived at but, for the general reader, I think the best answer is to browse through the sections until you get a feel for the way they are made up, so that when you try to make a specific identification you will know within a few pages where to start.

The photographs

The studio photographs of grasses and ferns were taken with a De Vere camera using a 210mm lens, strobe flash equipment and a 2 x 3ft Fish Fryer head, aperture f64. The studio close-ups of mosses and ferns were taken on a Nikkormat using a 105mm lens mounted on extension bellows, and aperture f22; the strobe lighting was the same as for the plate camera. The film stock was Kodak daylight Ektachrome 64 ASA. The location photographs were all taken in daylight using a Nikon F2 with an AS metering head which allowed me to take exposures up to 8 seconds. The lens was 55mm Micro Nikkor and the general run of exposures for the mosses was about 4 seconds at f22/32 to obtain as much depth of field as possible. The grasses and ferns, on the other hand, were shot with an exposure time of 1/15 secs and the best aperture possible which meant that the depth of field could not always be controlled, due to wind movement on the subject. The film used was Kodak daylight Ektachrome EPR 64 ASA. Although the faster film would have been useful for extra depth I rejected it as the colour saturation is not as good.

The shots that have been lent to me were all 35mm but using different sorts of stock, sometimes flash and sometimes daylight.

Grasses, sedges and rushes

This section comprises four botanical families: *Graminae* – grasses; *Cyperaceae* – sedges; *Juncaceae* – rushes; and *Typhaceae* – reedmaces.

Grasses make up the largest group. They are plants with long, narrow, parallel-veined leaves, hollow, rounded stems and small flowers enclosed by a pair of scales (glumes). These flowers are grouped together into spikelets – either singly, in pairs or several together and enclosed by another pair of scales. The spikelets are also arranged in a variety of ways – stalkless, in spikes or with long stalks in branched flowerheads. The glumes may sometimes have long, pointed projections known as awns, which can be useful in identification.

Sedges are similar but have solid, three-sided stems and leaves that form a continuous cylinder around the stem, unlike grass leaves which form a sheath by their edges overlapping. There are several different genera in this group, but all have flowers enclosed by glumes as in the grasses. The flowers are generally grouped into spikes, one or several of which make up the flowerhead. In the true sedges (*Carex*) which form the largest group in this family, the flowers are of one sex only and are often grouped into separate male and female spikes, which are easily distinguished by the males bearing pollen and the females swelling into small nuts as they ripen.

Rushes are similar to sedges, with solid or pithy, though not three-sided stems. The leaves also form continuous cylinders around the stem. The flowers are rather different, having a more conventional form, with six 'petals'. *Luzula* and *Juncus* are the two genera in this family.

Reedmaces are also included since they are so grass-like. They are in one genus only, *Typha*, and have unisexual flowers densely crowded in separate, velvety spikes on the same stem, the male cluster above the female.

Order in the book

The whole group has been arranged so that, as far as possible, similar looking plants are close together for easy comparison. The order also reflects a progression from simpler to more complex forms. Thus the sections start with the simple *Juncus* species (pp12-16), followed by the rush-like members of the sedge family (pp15-23), *Luzula* species (pp24-6), leading into *Carex* (pp26-37) which begin with the single-spiked species and progress to the multi-spiked species. The reedmaces are on pages 38 and 39. The grasses form the largest part of this section and are arranged as follows: the simple spikes (pp40-6); spike-like flowerheads where the spikelets are stalked and clustered to give the outward appearance of a spike (pp47-52); branched, open flowerheads with spikelets containing one flower (pp52-6); those with spikelets containing two flowers (pp57-9); those with spikelets containing three or more awnless flowers (pp60-7); those with spikelets containing three or more flowers with awns (pp68-73); branched open heads of flowers with long, bent awns (pp74-5).

The text

The captions supply the common and botanical names, followed by an abbreviation of the name of the person who first published the scientific name; the status – that is, whether native or introduced, and whether annual, biennial or perennial; habitat; dimensions; flowering time. Further details of the growth habit or of the plant's anatomy are described where useful for identification, particularly when they are not shown in the photograph. The date of photographing each specimen is also given. 162 plants are illustrated with photographs and many others are described to give a good coverage of the important species of grasses and grass-like plants.

Scientific names throughout follow *Flora of the British Isles*, by A. R. Clapham, T. G. Tutin and E. F. Warburg (see Further reading).

Ferns and fern allies

The plants in this group reproduce by spores, rather than by seed as in the more familiar flowering plants. They are the members of three botanical orders: *Filicopsida* – ferns; *Sphenopsida* – horsetails; *Lycopsida* – clubmosses and quillworts.

Fern leaves are commonly known as fronds and are tightly coiled when young, unwinding the coil as they expand. Spores are produced on the undersides of fronds (exceptions are pillwort and azolla) in structures called sori which are clusters of spore-producing sacs. They are formed vegetatively from the parent plant, that is, without sexual fertilization, being more like the removal of a cutting from a shrub or houseplant. When the spores fall on to wet ground they develop into small heart-shaped structures, about 0.5cm across, called prothalli, which contain male and female reproductive structures. In the wet conditions male cells migrate through the film of water on the plant's surface to the female receptacle. This part of the process is equivalent to pollination in flowering plants which would then produce seed. In the ferns a new fern plant grows directly from the fertilized female structure on the prothallus. When identifying ferns it is best to have sori on the specimen as their shape and structure provide the only sure identification in most instances. However, with practice it is often easy to recognize or at least place many ferns in their correct groups, using general characteristics such as leaf shape, texture and habitat.

Horsetails produce spores in cone-like structures at stem tips. The spores develop into lobed, underground prothalli which produce new plants in the same manner as the fern prothalli.

The horsetails are now represented by only one genus, *Equisetum*, but hundreds of millions of years ago they made up a large and important group of plants with tree-sized species growing in great forests. It is from these forests that coal was formed.

Clubmosses are an ancient group represented today by a few species. They are small, creeping plants with branched stems and leaves. Spores are produced in spore cases in the axils of the upper leaves and develop into prothalli underground in close association with soil fungi.

Quillworts are a small, unique group, with round, grass-like leaves in tufts and spores produced in structures hidden among the leaf bases. They are either aquatic or grow submerged in mud.

Order in the book

The different groups described above will be found separately, beginning with the ferns themselves. These are placed in their botanical genera, which are then ordered in a visual manner. The section begins with Lady Fern, *Athyrium filix-femina* (pp76-7), which is one of the most common of ferns and one of the large-fronded species so easily confused by the beginner. The other large-fronded ferns follow closely (pp78-93) in order to show how different they really are. These are followed by Bracken, *Pteridium aquilinum* (p94), Oak Fern and Limestone Fern (p96) which all have branched fronds, then by the *Asplenium* group (pp97-101) which are all relatively small and many of which are divided into tiny leaflets. Ferns with two different types of fronds appear next (pp102-4), followed by all the small, rare or untypical ferns (pp105-9). The horsetails (pp110-14), clubmosses (pp115-17) and quillworts (p115) are shown at the end of the section.

The text

The captions provide the common name(s) and botanical name, followed by the abbreviated name of the scientist who first published that name. As there have been so many nomenclatural changes in this group in recent years, previous scientific names still in use are given as synonyms. Rarity – an important factor with ferns since the Victorian fern craze led to the depletion of many wild populations – is described, as are habitat, dimensions, spore-producing structures, and sporing times. Other useful details are included where relevant and the date of photographing each specimen is given. Fifty-eight plants have been photographed for this section, giving a comprehensive coverage of ferns and their allies. Nomenclature throughout follows the *Atlas of British Ferns*, edited by A. C. Jermy.

Mosses and liverworts

These plants reproduce by spores, as do the fern group, but have a simpler structure. They have stems and leaves but no roots, only modified stems forming root-like structures known as rhizoids. Botanically they make up an order called *Bryophyta* and are classified into two groups: *Musci* – mosses; and *Hepaticae* – liverworts.

Mosses produce spores in capsules which may either eject them forcibly through a small opening when ripe (sphagnum), release them through four slits (*Andraea*) or, as in the majority of mosses, through an opening or mouth exposed when a lid drops off. On the ground they develop into new plants, not into prothalli as in ferns. The plant contains the male and female sexual structures, which are minute and often difficult to find, but may also be quite obvious as with the clusters of male structures in *Polytrichum* species. Male and female may be close together on the same plant but may also occur on separate plants, characteristics which vary with the species. Male cells migrate through the water film on the plant's surface to the female structure which has been found to secrete a chemical to guide them. Thus, as with ferns, damp conditions are essential to the sexual process. Once fertilized in this way the female receptacle develops a capsule which in turn produces spores.
Mosses have leaves in spirals or sometimes in two flat rows.
Liverworts are either flat-lobed structures or have small leaves in rows of three. These have a similar life cycle to mosses and the male and female structures are often quite obvious on the lobed types. The capsules differ from moss capsules by breaking open into four flaps, releasing the ripe spores.

Order in the book
Mosses are shown graduating from the simpler forms to the more complex, by loosely dividing them into four groups: those with upright stems (pp118-38); those with upright stems and clusters of branches at the apex (p139); those with creeping or ascending branched stems (pp140-51); *Sphagnum* with upright stems bearing whorls of leafy branches (pp152-5). The liverworts are divided into the flat-lobed types (pp156-9) and the leafy types (pp159-63). Many species are illustrated by two photographs: a location shot, showing the habitat and appearance in the field; and a detail of part of the plant.

The text
The captions give the botanical names and abbreviations of the authority who first published that name (common names for mosses and liverworts are few and rarely used); dimensions; habitat; details of the spore capsules; sporing times. Other characteristics useful for identification are discussed where relevant. The photographs are dated.
Nearly 140 species out of the total British *bryophyte* flora of around 1,000 have been described. Those included are the most common or noticeable members of the group.
Nomenclature for mosses follows *The Moss Flora of Britain and Ireland*, by A. J. E. Smith. For liverworts *British Mosses and Liverworts*, by E. V. Watson was used.

Lichens

Lichen plants consist of a fungus growing in close association (symbiosis) with an alga. They are commonly reproduced by vegetative means, fragments, usually specialized structures, dropping off and forming new plants. These fragments contain cells of both the fungal and algal partners. The fungal partner may sometimes produce spores in structures, called ascocarps, which may often be most noticeable on the surface of the plant. These spores contain only fungus cells, and it is believed that if they are to reproduce the lichen they must encounter cells of the alga wherever they land.

The process is a complex one and not yet fully understood.

Most lichens are highly sensitive to air pollution and to levels of sulphur dioxide in particular. Very few are found near centres of industry or in large towns and cities. This is obvious if you think of the bare tree-barks in woodland near London and the trees of a Scottish oakwood covered with hanging, grey tresses.

Country folk have traditionally used lichens for dyeing wool. This has been mentioned in the text where relevant, but remember lichens are extremely slow growing, so please do not gather them unless you find them in great abundance.

Order in the book
The lichens are arranged with the simplest looking forms first, graduating towards the more complex forms. There are five groups: the crust-like lichens, which form flat patches on rocks and trees (pp164-71); flat, lobed lichens (pp172-8); *Cladonia* and *Stereocaulon*, which are generally composed of scale-like structures giving rise to upright stems which may be branched or unbranched and often are swollen or cup-shaped towards the tips (pp178-83); the semi-erect, shrubby lichens with branched stems and no basal scales (pp183-4); the erect or hanging, shrubby lichens with branched stems but no basal scales (pp185-7).

The text
Captions give the common name (though very few exist); the botanical name, followed by the name of the authority who first published it; appearance; habitat; reproductive structures. Other useful pointers for identification are given where relevant.

Nearly 1,400 lichens have been recognized in the British Isles, of which no more than ninety-six species have been included here. These are the most common, noticeable or important. Lichens have rarely been illustrated in the past and there is next to nothing that you may refer to with photographs, but as you will see even my collection is only just scratching the surface of this vast subject.

Nomenclature throughout follows an updated *Checklist of British Lichens*, as used at the British Museum (Natural History).

Plant protection

Now that more and more people are able to reach our countryside by car, there is a greater danger to the rare and, come to that, the not so rare plants as well. Some, the *Woodsia* ferns for instance, are protected by law, the Protection of Wild Plants and Animals Act (1975); but I feel that the only real protection is for people to learn about them and come to love them so that they protect, and are thoughtful towards them instinctively.

Glossary

acid soil soil containing an excess of hydrogen ions, often found in areas where high rainfall leaches out the salts. Typical of moorland.

alga (plural **algae**) a large group of primitive plants which includes seaweeds.

annual a plant which completes its life cycle in one year.

anther the part of the flower which produces the pollen.

apothecium (plural **apothecia**) an open, spore-containing structure in lichens and some fungi.

appressed closely pressed to the substratum but not united with it.

auricle a small claw- or ear-like outgrowth at the junction of leaf sheaths and blades of some grasses.

awn a bristly process, such as the beard of barley.

base-rich soil soil containing an excess of basic ions, such as calcium or magnesium. Typical of the chalk or limestone downs of England, but may also occur in locally enriched places, such as around springs.

biconvex convex on both sides.

biennial a plant which completes its life cycle within two years, usually flowering in the second year.

blanket bog an area of bog covering like a blanket an entire surface, including small hills, not just hollows and valley bottoms.

bog a wet acid peat habitat with a characteristic *Sphagnum* moss vegetation.

bract a small (often modified) leaf that bears a flower or flowerhead in its axil.

bryophyte refers to members of the order *Bryophyta*, mosses and liverworts.

calcareous chalky or limy.

capsule the spore-bearing part of a moss, usually a pod-like structure on a slender stalk.

convex rising into a round form on the outside.

crenulate finely notched.

culm a grass or sedge stem.

deciduous sheds all its leaves annually, or may refer to other plant parts liable to be shed at a certain time.

decumbent lying flat with a rising tip.

dune low hill of wind-blown sand near the sea.

dune slack damp hollow between dunes.

flush watery place around a spring, often base-enriched.

frond a leaf, especially of a fern.

gemma (plural **gemmae**) a small, multicellular body, produced vegetatively, capable of separating and becoming a new individual.

genus (plural **genera**) a taxonomic group of closely related species.

glaucous covered with a fine greenish or bluish bloom.

glume an outer sterile bract which, alone or with others, encloses the spikelet in grasses and sedges.

hybrid a plant arising from the fertilization of one species by another.

inflorescence the whole flowering part of a plant.

isidium (plural **isidia**) a minute outgrowth which may become detached and serve as a reproductive structure.

leaflet leaf-like parts of a compound leaf.

ligule a scale at the top of a leaf sheath in grasses. (May also be a ring of hairs.)

lobe a broad, especially rounded, segmental division.

native not introduced by man.

node a place, often swollen, where a leaf is attached to a stem.

perennial a plant which lives for more than two years.

perianth calyx and corolla together, that is, the sepals and petals.

pinna (plural **pinnae**) leaflet of a pinnate leaf.

pinnate referring to a compound leaf with two rows of leaflets on either side of a central stem. **doubly pinnate** referring to a leaf with two rows of pinnate branches on either side of a central stem.

pinnule a lobe of a leaflet of a pinnate leaf.

prothallus (plural **prothalli**) a small plate of tissue derived from a spore and bearing male and female reproductive structures.

rhizinae hair-like organs of attachment on the lower part of a lichen thallus.

rhizoid hair-like organ on lower part of a liverwort or moss.

rhizome an underground organ formed from a swollen stem which lasts for more than one year and produces roots and leafy stock.

scree a mass of stones or fragments of rocks produced by the weathering of cliffs or rocks above.

sheath a clasping leaf base.

siliceous of, or containing silica. Siliceous rock forms an acid rather than alkaline substrate for mosses and lichens.

soredium (plural **soredia**) a small vegetative reproductive body in lichens, consisting of a few algal cells enclosed in fungal hyphae.

sorus (plural **sori**) a cluster of sporangia or soredia.

spike an inflorescence in which sessile flowers or spikelets are arranged on a long axis.

spikelet a small, crowded spike, itself forming part of a greater inflorescence.

sporangium (plural **sporangia**) a spore case or sac in which the spores are produced.

spore a unicellular, asexual, reproductive body.

squamulose composed of small scales.

stigma the female part of a flower which receives the pollen.

stolon a shoot from the base of a plant rooting and budding at the nodes.

thallus a plant body not differentiated into leaf, stem and root.

tomentose covered by a matted, cottony pubescence.

vegetative reproduction or **propagation** asexual reproduction by detachment of some part of the plant, rather than by specialized sexual reproductive organs.

Further reading

General

Flora of the British Isles, by A. R. Clapham, T. G. Tutin and E. F. Warburg (Cambridge University Press, 2nd edition, 1962)

The Oxford Book of Flowerless Plants, by F. H. Brightman and B. E. Nicholson (Oxford University Press, 1966)

Grasses, sedges and rushes

Grasses, by C. E. Hubbard (Penguin, 2nd edition, 1968)

Grasses, by Jaromir Sikula (Hamlyn, 1978)

The Observer's Book of Grasses, Sedges and Rushes, by W. J. Stokoe (Warne, 1958)

British Sedges, by A. C. Jermy and T. G. Tutin (Botanical Society of the British Isles, 1968)

Ferns and their allies

Atlas of Ferns of the British Isles, edited by A. C. Jermy (Botanical Society of the British Isles and British Pteridological Society, 1978)

The Observer's Book of Ferns, by W. J. Stokoe (Warne, 1961)

Welsh Ferns, by H. A. Hyde and A. E. Wade (National Museum of Wales, 6th edition, 1978)

Mosses and liverworts

British Mosses and Liverworts, by E. V. Watson (Cambridge University Press, 1968)

The Moss Flora of Britain and Ireland, by A. J. E. Smith (Cambridge University Press, 1978)

Lichens

A new checklist of British Lichens, by P. W. James (British Lichen Society, 1966)

Introduction to British Lichens, by U. K. Duncan (Buncle, 1970)

Lichens for Vegetable Dyeing, by Eileen Bolton (Studio Vista, 1960)

The Observer's Book of Lichens, by Kenneth L. Alvin (Warne, 1977)

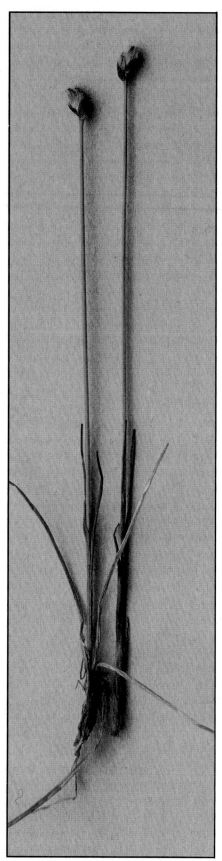

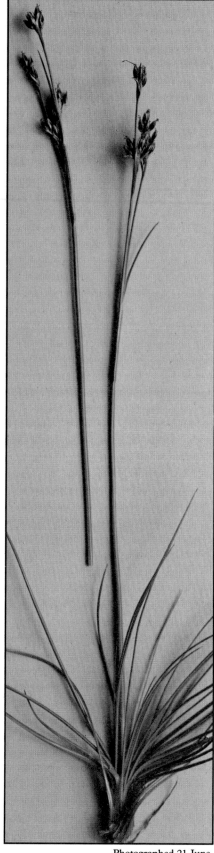

Photographed 22 June

Photographed 6 September

Photographed 21 June

Three-flowered Rush *Juncus triglumis* L.
Native perennial, found on bogs and rock ledges
on mountains above 300m. Most frequent in
Scotland, also found in Wales and the Lake
District. Height from 5 to 10cm. Flowers June
to July.
Two-flowered Rush *J. biglumis* L. is smaller,
grows in Scotland on mountains above 600m.
Height from 5 to 12cm. Flowers June to July.

Toad Rush *Juncus bufonius* L. Native annual,
common throughout Britain on cultivated land,
roadsides and muddy places by ponds and
rivers. It is short and branched from near the
base. Height from 3 to 25cm. Flowers May to
September.

Heath Rush *Juncus squarrosus* L. Native
perennial, forming dense tufts easily recognized
by the rosette of leaves strongly bent back
against the ground and the straight, tough
flowering stem in the centre. Common on acid
soils on moorland heaths and bogs, especially
where sheep grazing is heavy, uncommon in
south England. Height from 15 to 50cm.
Flowers June to July.

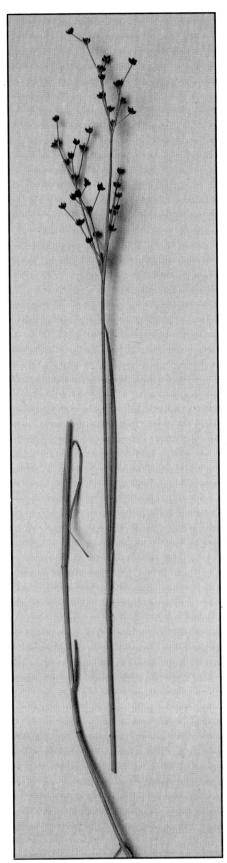

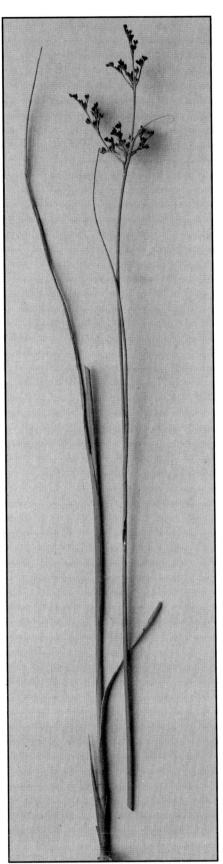

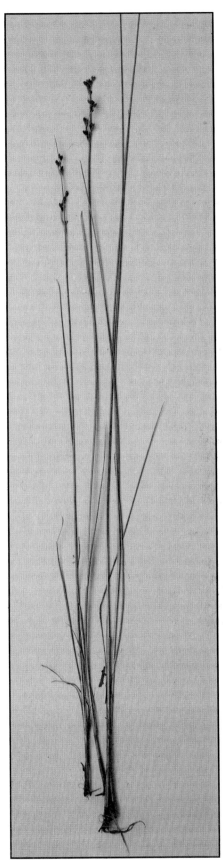

Photographed 25 July

Photographed 19 August

Photographed 29 June

Jointed Rush *Juncus articulatus* L. Native perennial with rhizomes, usually prostrate or rising from a bent base. Similar to the Sharp-flowered Rush but common throughout Britain on wet acid soils, usually on grazed areas. Height from 30 to 80cm. Flowers June to September.

Sharp-flowered Rush *Juncus acutiflorus* Ehrh. ex Hoffm. Native perennial with long rhizomes; common throughout Britain on wet moorland, woodland and meadows, particularly on acid soil. The flowers are chestnut-brown, the fruit tapers to a sharp point and the leaves have between eighteen and twenty-five horizontal thickened partitions in the pith. Flowers July to September.

Mud Rush *Juncus gerardii* Lois. Native perennial forming tufts and spreading by long rhizomes. Common in salt marshes near the high-tide mark on all coasts of Britain. Height from 25 to 40cm. Flowers June to July.

Three-leaved Rush *J. trifidus* L. grows on rock ledges on mountain-tops and has few flowers grouped at the base of long stem leaves. Height to 15cm. Flowers June to August.

Photographed 29 June

Juncus kochii Photographed 29 June

Juncus kochii F. W. Schultz. Native perennial found throughout Britain in wet places on heaths, bogs and in open woods on acid soil. The stem base is bulb-shaped. Height from 15 to 30cm. Flowers June to September.
Bulbous Rush *J. bulbosus* L. is similar but more common and forms dense tufts in similar habitats. The stem base is narrower and height is 10 to 20cm. Flowers June to September.

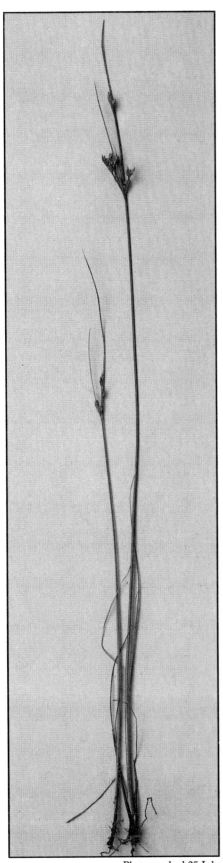

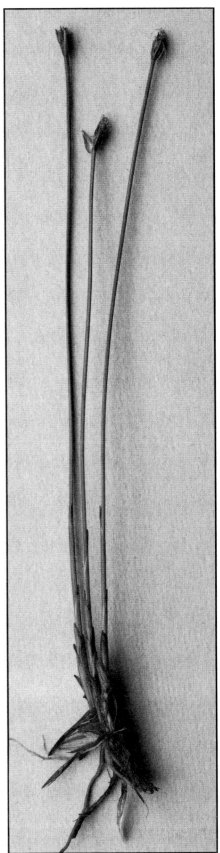

Photographed 25 July

Photographed 29 June

Photographed 31 May

Round-fruited Rush *Juncus compressus* Jacq. Native perennial with short rhizomes. Uncommon; found on marshes and wet meadows which have been grazed or mown and usually on non-acid soil. Most frequent in the south and east of England, rare elsewhere. Distinguished by its narrow flattened leaves. Height from 10 to 30cm. Flowers June to July.

Hard Rush *Juncus inflexus* L. Native perennial forming large tufts with thick matted rhizomes. It is hard dark bluish-green and ridged. Poisonous to livestock. Height from 25 to 60cm. Flowers June to August. *J. acutus* L. and *J. maritimus* Lam. grow on salt marshes and dune slacks; *J. acutus* is densely tufted and prickly, *J. maritimus* bright green and much branched.

Deer-grass *Trichophorum cespitosum* (L.) Hartm., synonym *Scirpus cespitosus* L. Native perennial, forming dense tufts, common on bogs, wet heaths and hill grassland throughout upland Britain. The upper leaf sheath is prolonged into a short bristle-like blade which helps in recognizing this species. Height from 5 to 25cm. Flowers May to June. Fruits July to August.

15

Soft Rush *Juncus effusus* Photographed 4 July

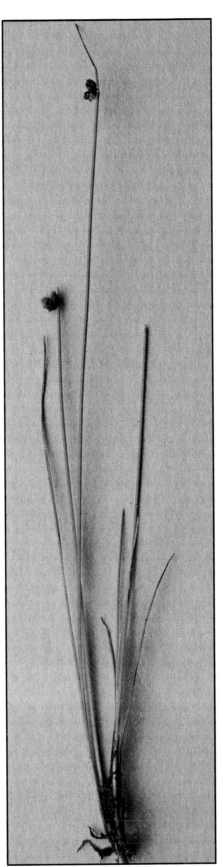

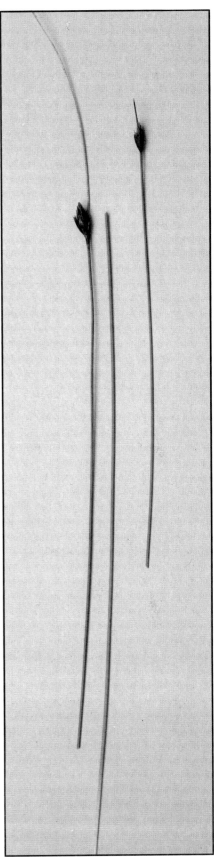

Photographed 4 July

Photographed 25 July

Photographed 29 June

Soft Rush *Juncus effusus* L. Native perennial forming thick tufts, common throughout Britain in bogs, wet woods and pasture. Differs from Hard Rush by being softer, smooth and light yellowish green. Height from 30 to 150cm. Flowers June to August.
J. conglomeratus L. grows in similar habitats, but the flowers form a small rounded head and the stem is ridged. Flowers May to July.

Bristle Scirpus *Isolepis setacea* (L.) R. Br., synonym *Scirpus setaceus* L. Native perennial, forming small tufts in damp meadows and wet flushes, throughout Britain. Height from 2 to 15cm. Flowers May to July. Fruits June to September.
Nodding Scirpus *I. cernua* (Vahl) Roem. & Schult. is similar with shorter bracts; less common and found near the sea.

Bog-rush *Schoenus nigricans* L. Native perennial found in wet peaty, base-rich places, usually near the sea. Most common in the north and west of Scotland and west of Ireland, scattered elsewhere. Height from 15 to 75cm. Flowers May to June. Fruits July to August.

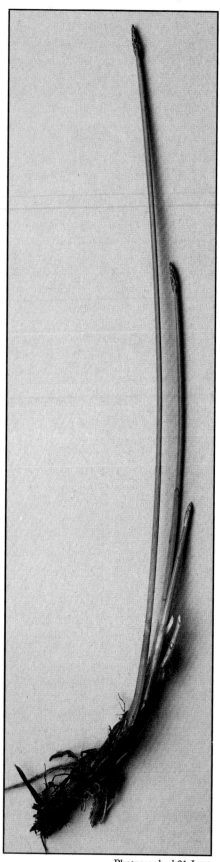

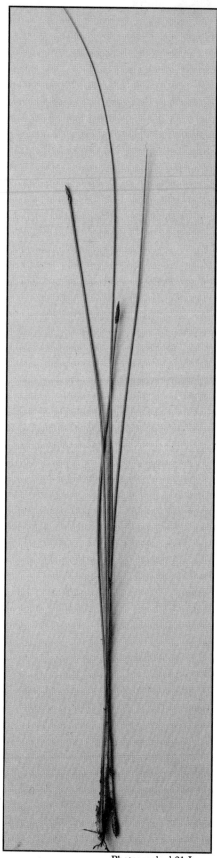

Photographed 21 June

Photographed 17 August

Photographed 21 June

Common Spike-rush *Eleocharis palustris* (L.) Roem. & Schult. Native perennial, fairly common throughout Britain, growing in marshy ground, lake and pond edges and wet meadows. Height is usually between 10 and 60cm. The plant forms a far-reaching rhizome which produces single stems or small tufts. The fruit is biconvex and yellowish brown. Flowers May to July, fruits June to August.

Few-flowered Spike-rush *Eleocharis quinqueflora* (F. X. Hartmann) Schwartz. Native perennial, tufted, with short thick rhizomes which produce long runners. Most common in the west and north of Scotland on damp peaty places and wet flushes; and scattered through the rest of Britain on similar habitats and fens. Height from 5 to 30cm. Flowers June to July. Fruits July to August.

One-glumed Spike-rush *Eleocharis uniglumis* (Link) Schult. Native perennial, found in marshes especially near the coast. Very similar to the Common Spike-rush but the lowest glume is larger and completely surrounds the spike. Height from 10 to 60cm. Flowers May to July.

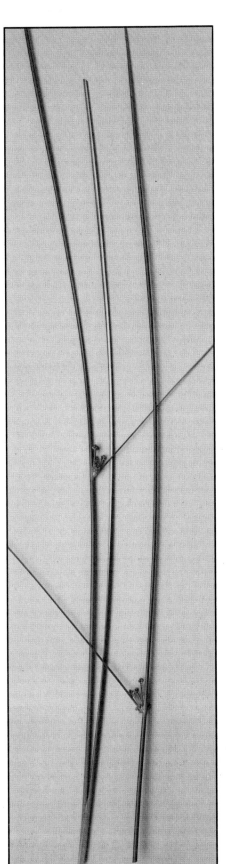

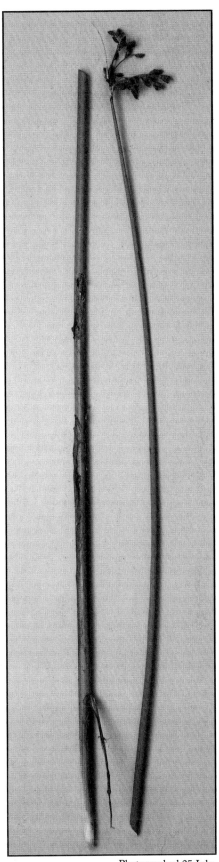

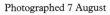

Photographed 7 August

Photographed 12 July

Photographed 25 July

Galingale *Cyperus longus* L. Native perennial, found in marshes and ditches and by ponds in scattered localities in Wales and the south of England. In North America Galingale is used for basket-weaving and paper-making. Height from 50 to 100cm. Flowers August to September.

Round-headed Club-rush *Holoschoenus vulgaris* Link, synonym *Scirpus holoschoenus* L. Native perennial, rare and found only on a few damp sandy places near the sea in north Devon, north Somerset and Glamorgan. Height from 50 to 100cm. Flowers July to August.

Bulrush *Schoenoplectus lacustris* (L.) Palla, synonym *Scirpus lacustris* L. Native perennial which grows in silty lakes, rivers and ponds throughout Britain but most common in the south and east of England and in Ireland. Dried stems are used for matting and thatching, and the pith has been used in making paper. Height from 100 to 300cm. Flowers June to July. Fruits August to September.

Glaucous Bulrush *Schoenoplectus tabernaemontani* Photographed 29 June

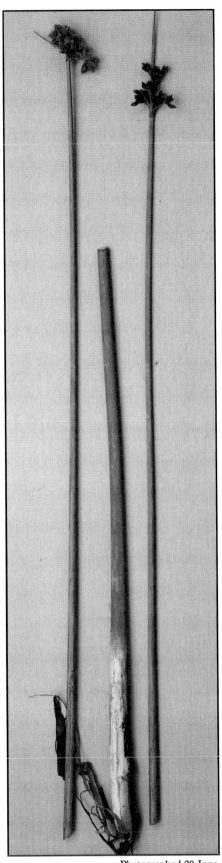

Photographed 29 June

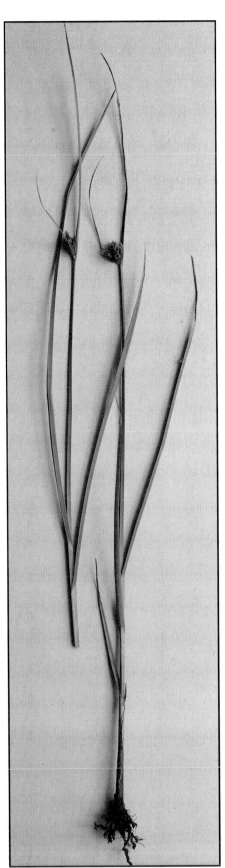

Photographed 16 July

Photographed 7 June

Glaucous Bulrush *Schoenoplectus tabernaemontani* (C.C. Gmel.) Palla, synonym *Scirpus tabernaemontani* C.C. Gmel. Native perennial, growing in streams, ditches and pools, often on peaty soil, usually near the sea. Found on most coasts though less frequent in the north. The stems are glaucous blue. Height from 50 to 150cm. Flowers June to July. Fruits August to September.

Sea Club-rush *Scirpus maritimus* L. Native perennial with creeping rhizomes which grows by tidal rivers and in salt marsh ponds and ditches usually in shallow water. Found on most British coasts in suitable habitats. Height from 30 to 100cm. Flowers July to August. Fruits August to September.

Wood Club-rush *Scirpus sylvaticus* L. Native perennial with creeping rhizomes, found in marshes and wet ground in woods, scattered throughout Britain though less common in the north of Scotland and Ireland. Height from 30 to 100cm. Flowers June to July. Fruits July to August.

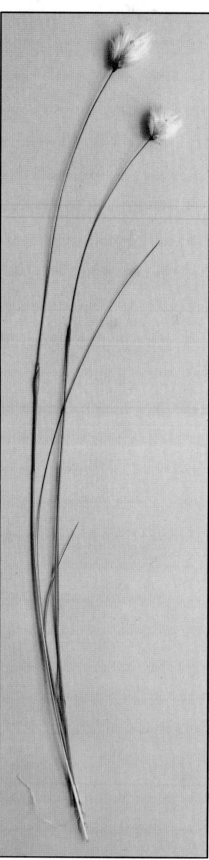

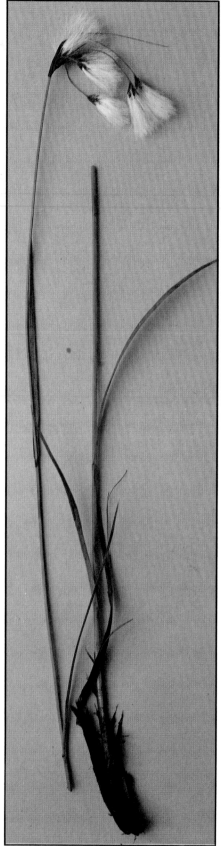

Photographed 12 June

Photographed 21 June

Photographed 6 August

Broad Blysmus *Blysmus compressus* (L.) Panz. ex Link. Native perennial, found on marshy ground, scattered throughout England and the south of Scotland. Height from 10 to 35cm. Flowers June to July. Fruits August to September. **Narrow Blysmus** *B. rufus* (Huds.) Link has narrow leaves, between five and eight brown spikelets in the flowerhead and grows in salt marshes, more frequent in the north.

Cotton-grass or **Hare's-tail** *Eriophorum vaginatum* L. Native perennial which grows in tussocks and spreads by rhizomes. Found on wet peaty soils, particularly blanket bogs, where it forms part of the characteristic vegetation. Easily distinguished from the other Cotton-grasses by single flower-spikes. Height from 30 to 50cm. Flowers April to May. Fruits May to June.

Broad-leaved Cotton-grass *Eriophorum latifolium* Hoppe. Native perennial, growing in small tufts in wet places, usually on base-rich soils or flushes (other Cotton-grasses grow on acid substrate). Uncommon, but most frequent in the Scottish highlands. Leaves are flat, not keeled, as on Common Cotton-grass. Height from 20 to 60cm. Flowers May to June. Fruits June to August.

Common Cotton-grass *Eriophorum angustifolium* Photographed 31 May

Photographed 31 May

Common Cotton-grass *Eriophorum angustifolium* Honck. Native perennial with creeping rhizomes, common in wettest parts of bogs and acid fen. Height from 20 to 60cm. The keeled leaves are about 0.5cm wide and form a long three-sided point at the tip. Flowers May to June. Fruits June to July.

Photographed 5 June

Photographed 5 May

Photographed 12 June

Forster's Woodrush *Luzula forsteri* (Sm.) DC. Native tufted perennial, found in woodland and hedgerows in the south of England and Wales. The flowerhead branches droop slightly to one side but remain more or less upright when fruiting. Height from 10 to 25cm. Flowers April to June.

Hairy Woodrush *Luzula pilosa* (L.) Willd. Native perennial with stolons. Common in woods and hedgerows throughout Britain, though uncommon in Ireland. Some of the flowerhead branches are strongly curved back downwards when fruiting. Height from 15 to 30cm. Flowers April to June.

Luzula luzuloides (Lam.) Dandy & Wilmott. Introduced perennial, naturalized in a few scattered places throughout Britain in damp woods or by streams usually on acid soils. Flowers are whitish, tinged red or pink. Height from 30 to 60cm. Flowers June to July.

Greater Woodrush *Luzula sylvatica* Photographed 12 June

Photographed 12 June

Greater Woodrush *Luzula sylvatica* (Huds.)
Gaud. Native perennial, forming large
tussocks, and spreading by stolons. Common
on the acid soils of north and west Britain in
woods and on moors. The leaves are much
longer, broader and glossier than other
Woodrushes. Height from 30 to 80cm.
Flowers May to June.

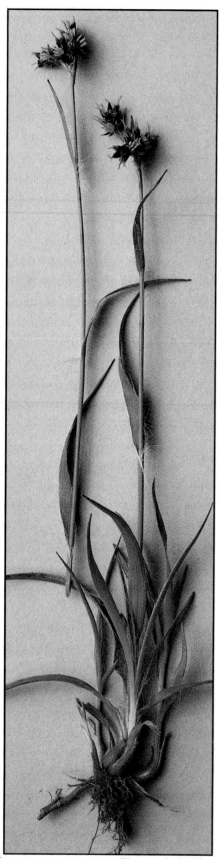

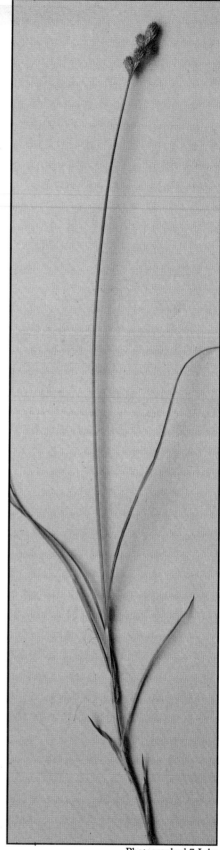

Photographed 5 May

Photographed 31 May

Photographed 7 July

Field Woodrush or **Sweep's Brush** *Luzula campestris* (L.) DC. Native perennial, with short stolons, common throughout Britain on all types of grassland, lawns or fields. The flowerheads consist of one stemless cluster and from three to six stemmed spherical clusters. Height from 5 to 15cm. Flowers March to June.

Many-headed Woodrush *Luzula multiflora* (Retz.) Lej. Native perennial, usually with no stolons. Common throughout Britain on moorland, heath and woodland particularly on acid or peaty soil. Similar to Field Woodrush, but has from eight to sixteen ovate, stalked or sessile flower clusters and has a later flowering period. Height from 20 to 40cm. Flowers April to June.

Oval Sedge *Carex ovalis* Good. Native perennial, forming tufts in wet meadows, open woodland and heaths on poorly drained acid soils. Fairly common throughout Britain, less frequent in east England and south-east Ireland. Height from 10 to 90cm. Flowers June. Fruits July to August.

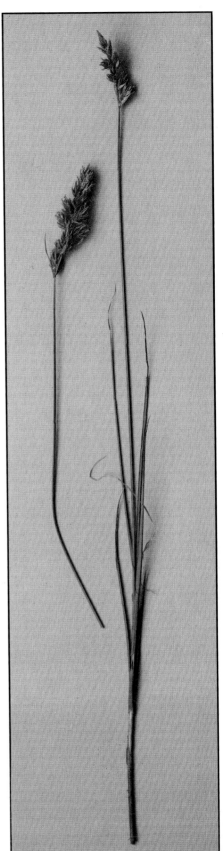

Photographed 29 June

Photographed 28 June

Photographed 26 June

Sand Sedge *Carex arenaria* L. Native perennial, common on fixed sand dunes around all British coasts and found on a few sandy heaths inland. Long rhizomes creep along the surface of the sand, joining plants in far reaching rows. Height 10 to 40cm. Flowers June to July. Fruits July to August.

Brown Sedge *C. disticha* Huds. grows in fens and wet meadows. It is taller and more slender.

False Fox Sedge *Carex otrubae* Podp. Native perennial forming dense tufts, found in ditches and damp grassland on heavy clay soils, most common in the Midlands and south England, scattered through Ireland and only on coastal areas elsewhere. Height from 30 to 100cm. Flowers June to July. Fruits July to September.

Greater Tussock Sedge *Carex paniculata* L. Native perennial forming large thick tussocks, up to 100cm in height and width. Found in damp peaty base-rich places, often in the shade of alders. Most common in England and Wales, scattered in Ireland and rare in Scotland. Height from 60 to 150cm. Flowers May to June. Fruits June to August.

Photographed 20 June

Photographed 28 June

Photographed 5 June

Spiked Sedge *Carex spicata* Huds. Native perennial forming dense tufts, found in marshes, ditches, hedgerows on base-rich soils. Common in south and east England, scattered and rare elsewhere. Flowers May to June. Fruits June to July.

Divided Sedge *Carex divisa* Huds. Native perennial with thick woody creeping rhizomes, uncommon, found in marshes or damp pasture often with Common Reed; frequent in the south and east of England, scattered or rare elsewhere. The flowerhead is usually dark brownish-purple and has a long stiff bract at its base. Height from 15 to 80cm. Flowers May to June. Fruits July to August.

Grey Sedge *Carex divulsa* Stokes. Native perennial, forming dense tufts. It is found throughout England and Wales; though more common in the south, in hedgerows, pasture and waste ground. Height from 25 to 75 cm. It forms thick tufts. Flowers June to July. Fruits July to August.

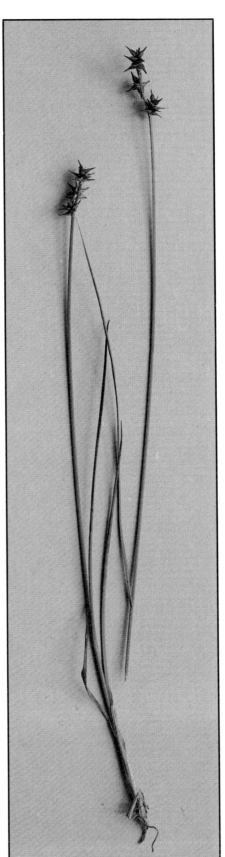

Photographed 30 June

Photographed 29 June

Photographed 22 June

Remote Sedge *Carex remota* L. Native perennial forming dense tussocks in damp woods and other shady places, often in alder or birch woods. Found throughout Britain but rare in north Scotland. The widely separated short flower spikes and long bracts make this sedge easily recognized. Height from 30 to 75cm. Flowers June. Fruits June to August.

Star Sedge *Carex echinata* Murr. Native perennial forming dense tufts, common on wet moorland and bogs on acid peaty soils throughout the British Isles though less common in central and eastern England. Distinctive due to its ripe fruits forming a star-shaped spike. Height from 10 to 40cm. Flowers May to June. Fruits June to August.

Flea Sedge *Carex pulicaris* L. Native perennial forming dense tufts, found in wet calcareous grassland or base-rich flushes on hillsides. Most common in Scotland and north England; uncommon in central and south England. The female flowers bend downwards when ripe. Height from 10 to 30cm. Flowers May to July. Fruits June to July.

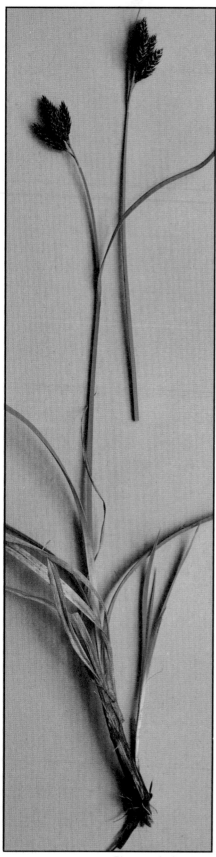

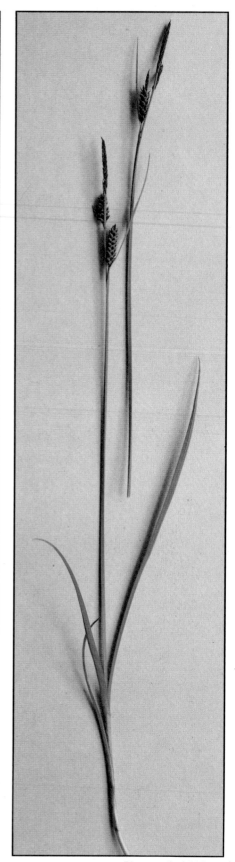

Photographed 22 June

Photographed 22 May

Photographed 21 June

Black Alpine Sedge *Carex atrata* L. Native perennial forming loose tufts. Rare, found only on wet cliff-ledges often on calcareous rocks at altitudes above 725m. Most frequent in Scotland; also found in the Lake District and north Wales. Height from 30 to 50cm. Flowers June to July. Fruits July to September.

Mountain Sedge *Carex montana* L. Native perennial with thick mat-forming rhizomes, growing in rough grassland usually on limestone rather than on mountains as its name suggests. Uncommon and found in scattered localities in south England and south Wales. Leaves are pale green. Height from 10 to 40cm. Flowers May. Fruits May to June.

Common Sedge *Carex nigra* (L.) Reich. Native perennial, usually with short creeping rhizomes. Common throughout Britain on bogs, marshes and damp grassland on both acid and basic soils. The fruits are enclosed by black glumes which give the ripe female spikes the appearance of being wholly black. Height from 7 to 70cm. Flowers May to July. Fruits June to August.

Hair Sedge *Carex capillaris* Photographed 5 July

Photographed 5 July

Hair Sedge *Carex capillaris* L. Native perennial, rare and local, forming small tufts on wet hillsides on base-rich soil in the Grampians, on limestone in the north of Scotland and a few other scattered places in Lancashire, Wales and the Scottish Borders. The photograph left shows flowers of *Silene acaulis* in the background. Height from 10 to 20cm. Flowers July. Fruits July to August.

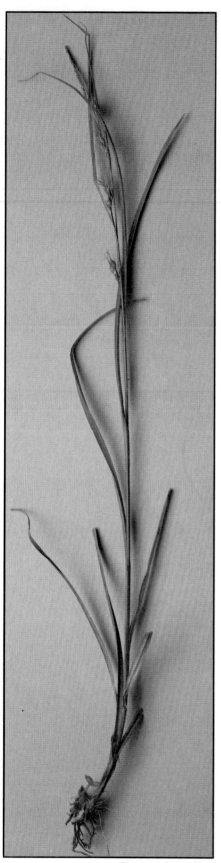

Photographed 7 June

Photographed 30 June

Photographed 22 June

Starved Wood Sedge *Carex depauperata*
Curt. ex With. Native perennial with creeping
rhizomes, very rare, found only in woods or
hedgerows on dry calcareous soils in Surrey,
Somerset, Anglesey and County Cork. Easily
recognized by its few-flowered (depauperate)
spikes with relatively large fruits. Height from
30 to 60cm. Flowers May. Fruits June to July.

Common Yellow Sedge *Carex demissa*
Hornem. Native perennial forming tufts,
common on damp grassland or bogs on acid
soils. The flowerhead has one stalked male
spike and two or three female spikes. Height
5 to 30cm. Flowers June. Fruits July to August.
Long-stalked Yellow Sedge *C. lepidocarpa*
Tausch is similar, but grows on base-rich soils
and has larger, longer-beaked fruits.

Pale Sedge *Carex pallescens* L. Native
perennial often forming large tufts in open
damp woods and sometimes on wet ledges on
hillsides. Most frequent in the west and south
of Scotland and scattered elsewhere. The leaves
are hairy underneath and on the sheath and the
lowest bract is distinctly crimped at its base.
Height from 20 to 60cm. Flowers May to June.
Fruits June to July.

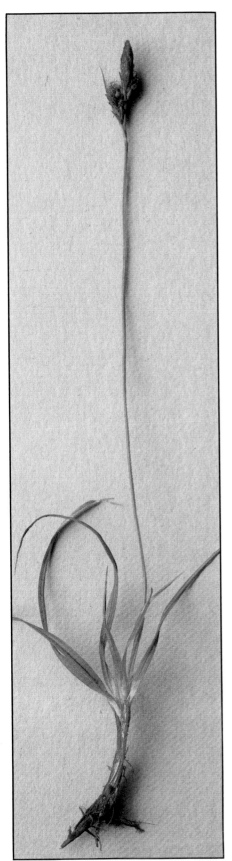

Photographed 30 May

Photographed 29 June

Photographed 6 June

Spring Sedge *Carex caryophyllea* Latour.
Native perennial with creeping rhizomes,
common on chalk or limestone grassland but
also on other dry grassland and basic flushes on
acid ground. Found throughout most of Britain
but rare in the north of Scotland. The fruit is
minutely downy. Height from 5 to 15cm.
Flowers April to May. Fruits May to July.

Distant Sedge *Carex distans* L. Native
perennial forming dense tufts, found
throughout the British Isles in marshes and wet
rocks near the sea though often inland in the
south and east of England. The leaves turn
brown, then grey, and persist through the
winter. Height from 15 to 45cm. Flowers May
to June. Fruits June to July.

Green-ribbed Sedge *Carex binervis* Smith.
Native, often forming dense clumps, common
on the acid soils of mountain grassland, and
sandy heaths in the lowlands. Uncommon in
the south and east of England. Most similar to
Distant Sedge but easily distinguished by its
ripe three-sided fruit having two dark green
nerves. Height from 30 to 60cm. Flowers
June. Fruits July.

33

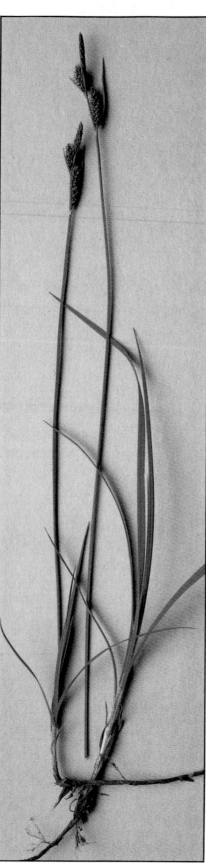

Photographed 2 June

Photographed 7 June

Photographed 5 June

Hairy Sedge or **Hammer Sedge** *Carex hirta* L. Native perennial with long rhizomes. Common in hedgerows, meadows, roadsides and sometimes damp woods throughout Britain but rare in high rainfall areas. The hairy sheaths, leaves and fruits are distinctive. Height from 15 to 70cm. Flowers May to June. Fruits June to July.

Downy-fruited Sedge *Carex filiformis* L. Native perennial; rare, found on damp meadows and roadsides in the south of England. Fruit is downy, unlike that of other sedges of similar size. Height from 20 to 50cm. Flowers May to June. Fruits June to July.
Slender Sedge *C. lasiocarpa* Ehrh. also has downy fruit, but is 45 to 120cm tall with longer spikes and grows in swamps.

Carnation Grass or **Glaucous Sedge** *Carex flacca* Schreb. Native perennial with creeping rhizomes, common throughout Britain on calcareous grassland, wet flushes, marshes, fens and bogs. The pale bluish-green leaves are similar in colour to carnation leaves, hence the English name. Height from 10 to 60cm. Flowers May to June. Fruits June to September.

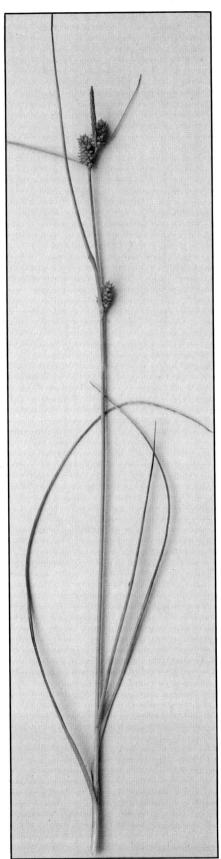

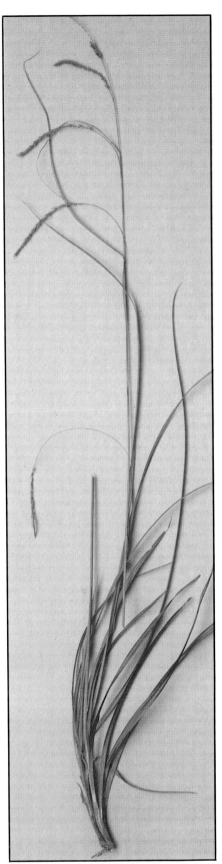

Photographed 29 June

Photographed 10 June

Photographed 7 July

Long-bracted Sedge *Carex extensa* Good.
Native perennial, forming tufts on muddy or
sandy ground near the sea, frequent on most
British and Irish coasts though rare in the east.
The long bracts below each flower spike are a
distinctive feature. Height from 20 to 40cm.
Flowers June to July. Fruits July to August.

Carnation Sedge *Carex panicea* L. Native
perennial with creeping rhizomes, common on
mountain grassland, marsh and fen. The blue
leaves are similar to Carnation Grass but it
has a sparser-fruiting spike and the leaf tip is
tapered to a three-sided point. The photograph
shows a greener specimen than is usual. Height
from 10 to 60cm. Flowers May to June. Fruits
June to September.

Wood Sedge *Carex sylvatica* Huds. Native
perennial, forming dense tufts in wet woods,
scrub and sometimes open grassland. Found
throughout most of Britain but rare in north
Scotland. The long, stalked, hanging female
spikes and its woodland habitat make it easily
recognized. Height from 15 to 60cm. Flowers
May to July. Fruits July to September.

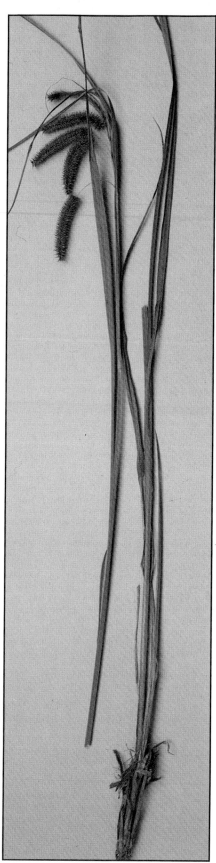

Photographed 10 June

Photographed 6 July

Photographed 7 July

Pendulous Sedge *Carex pendula* Huds.
Native perennial, forming a large tuft, in damp
deciduous woodland and beside shady streams;
most frequent on heavy clay soils in the south
and east of England. Easily recognized by its
large size and long pendulous female spikes.
Height from 60 to 180cm. Flowers May to
June. Fruits June to July.

Cyperus Sedge *Carex pseudocyperus* L. Native
perennial forming thick tufts in shallow slow-
moving water and swamps. Most frequent in
the south and east of England, rare in Wales,
Ireland and Scotland. The large hanging
female spikes are rough and bristly and this,
with the plant's yellowish-green colour make
it easily recognized. Height 40 to 90cm.
Flowers May to June. Fruits July to August.

Bladder Sedge *Carex vesicaria* L. Native
perennial with short creeping rhizomes, found
on lake, canal, river and streamsides and other
wet peaty places. Scattered throughout Britain,
though nowhere common. The leaf sheaths
become red and fibrous at the base,
distinguishing it from Bottle Sedge. Height from
30 to 120cm. Flowers June. Fruits July to August.

Greater Pond Sedge *Carex riparia* Photographed 7 June

Photographed 7 June

Greater Pond Sedge *Carex riparia* Curt.
Native perennial with long creeping rhizomes,
forming dense stands in ditches, by ponds and
rivers in wet meadows and marshes. Common
in south and east England, scattered elsewhere.
The upright growth habit and bluish leaves
distinguish it from Lesser Pond Sedge.
Height from 60 to 130cm. Flowers May to
June. Fruits June to August.

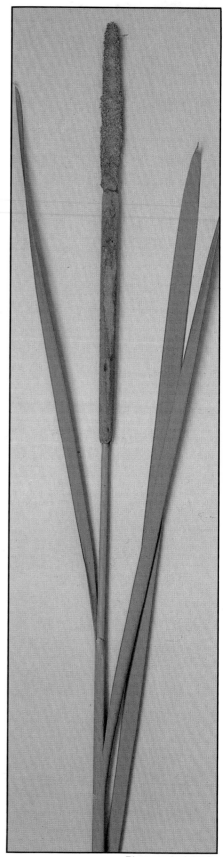

Photographed 7 June

Photographed 29 August

Photographed 4 July

Lesser Pond Sedge *Carex acutiformis* Ehrh.
Native perennial with creeping rhizomes,
growing in ditches, ponds, slow-moving rivers
often with Greater Pond Sedge. Common
throughout England, scattered elsewhere.
Height from 60 to 150cm. Flowers June to
July. Fruits July to August.

Bottle Sedge *Carex rostrata* Stokes. Native
perennial with long creeping rhizomes,
common in wet peaty areas by lakes, and in
swamps in north England and Scotland, also
found in acid fens in the south. Similar to the
Bladder Sedge but the fruit is shorter and more
abruptly tapered to a point and the stem bases
lack the fibrous sheaths. Height 20 to 100cm.
Flowers June to July. Fruits July to September.

Great Reedmace or **Cat's-tail** *Typha
latifolia* L. Native perennial with underwater
rhizomes, found in swamps, ditches, lakes and
slow-moving rivers and canals. Common
throughout England less frequent elsewhere.
The male and female clusters are not separated
by a length of stem. Height from 150 to 250cm.
Flowers June to July.

Lesser Reedmace *Typha angustifolia* Photographed 25 July

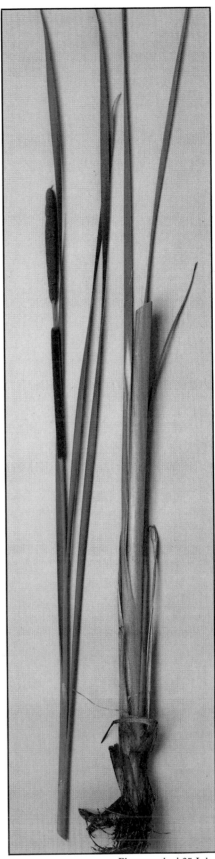

Photographed 25 July

Lesser Reedmace *Typha angustifolia* L.
Native perennial found in swamps, ditches,
lakes, ponds and slow-moving rivers. Locally
abundant in the south and east of England,
scattered or rare elsewhere. The male and
female flower clusters are between 1 and 9cm
apart on the flower spike, separated by a
length of green stem. Height from 100 to
300cm. Flowers June to July.

Photographed 5 June

Photographed 10 May

Photographed 28 June

Mat-grass *Nardus stricta* L. Native perennial which forms dense tufts. Common in the north and west, on heaths, moors and hill grassland. Unpalatable to sheep since it becomes hard and fibrous through the season, therefore dominant in much of our hill pasture. The small, hard tufts may be found uprooted and discarded on such areas. Height from 10 to 40cm. Flowers June to August.

Early Sand-grass or **Sand Bent** *Mibora minima* (L.) Desv. Native annual of damp, sandy ground near the sea on Anglesey and the Channel Isles, also found naturalized in Hampshire, Dorset and East Lothian. The earliest of grasses to flower and flowers again in late summer or autumn depending on the weather. Height from 2 to 15cm. Flowers February to May.

Sea Hard-grass *Parapholis strigosa* (Dum.) C.E. Hubbard. Native perennial, common on salt marshes and wasteland near the sea on most British coasts except in the north of Scotland. The stiff, flowering spikes are very narrow and may not be immediately recognized as flowerheads until one spots the yellow stamens. Height from 15 to 40cm. Flowers June to August.

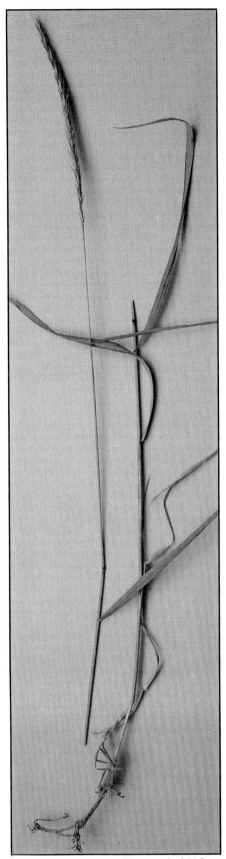

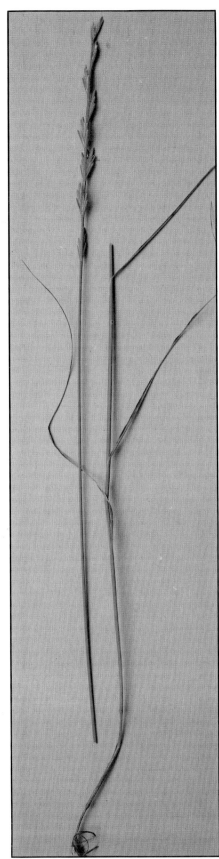

Photographed 26 June

Photographed 28 July

Photographed 10 July

Bearded Couch *Agropyron caninum* (L.) Beauv. Native perennial forming loose tufts. Common in shady places and woods in England, Wales and south Scotland, rare elsewhere. The long stem may be tinged purple and is usually curved or drooping. Easily distinguished by its long awns which give a bearded appearance. Height from 30 to 110cm. Flowers June to August.

Don's Twitch *Agropyron donianum* F.B. White. A very rare grass, found only on a few Scottish mountains in Sutherland and Perthshire, forming tufts in rock-clefts and cliffs, often near water. Height from 50 to 100cm. Flowers late July to August.

Sand Couch *Agropyron junceiforme* (A. & D. Love) A. & D. Love. Native perennial, found on sand dunes, on most British coasts, often the only grass on the younger dunes close to the sea and among Marram and Sand Fescue further back. Height from 20 to 60cm. Sand Couch spreads by its tough rhizomes which bind the loose dunes. Leaves are bluish-grey. Flowers June to August.

41

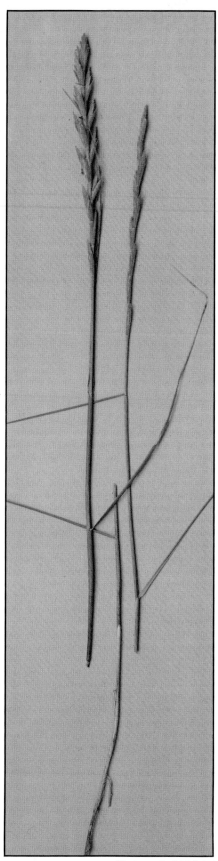

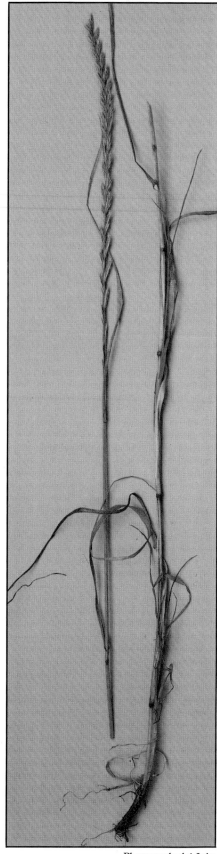

Photographed 10 July

Photographed 28 June

Photographed 4 July

Sea Couch *Agropyron pungens* (Pers.) Roem. & Schult. Native perennial, common on English and Welsh coasts, rare in Scotland and Ireland. It grows on sand dunes and at the edges of salt marshes. The whole plant is bluish in colour and spreads by means of creeping rhizomes. Individual spikes overlap each other, distinguishing it from Sand Couch. Height from 20 to 120cm. Flowers June to August.

Couch-grass or **Twitch** *Agropyron repens* (L.) Beauv. Native perennial, forming large tufts, common throughout Britain on waste-ground and arable land. Considered a persistent and annoying weed as it is almost impossible to eradicate; each fragment of rhizome is capable of producing a new plant. Many names exist in different parts of the country. Height from 30 to 120cm. Flowers June to August.

Italian Rye-grass *Lolium multiflorum* Lam. Annual or biennial, introduced in the early nineteenth century for fodder, naturalized on roadsides, waste-ground and field edges. Height from 30 to 100cm. Flowers June to August. **Darnel** *L. temulentum* L. looks similar but is now rare due to the diligence of farmers. It becomes infected by a fungus 'ergot' which causes blindness and abortion in cows.

42

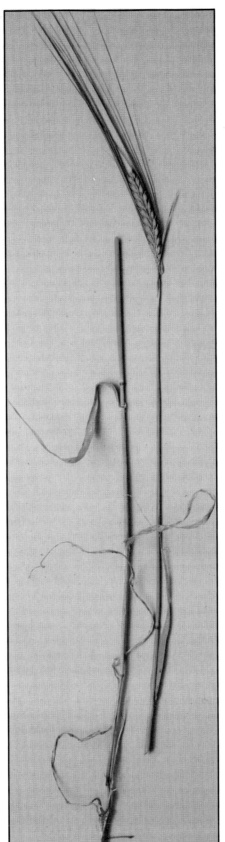

Photographed 5 June

Photographed 12 July

Photographed 12 July

Perennial Rye-grass *Lolium perenne* L.
Native perennial, long sown as a fodder crop,
for hay or for grazing. Common throughout
Britain on waste-ground, meadows, fields and
roadsides. Height from 10 to 90cm. Flowers
May to August.

Two-rowed Barley *Hordeum distichon* L.
The most commonly cultivated Barley in
Britain, many different varieties being available
to the farmer. Sometimes found as an escape or
relic of cultivation. Barley provides food for
livestock and man and the malt for brewing
beer.

Four-rowed Barley or **Six-rowed Barley**
Hordeum vulgare L. Less common in Britain
than Two-rowed Barley, but is also cultivated
for food and malt, and commonly grown in the
rest of Europe. Rarely naturalized but
sometimes found as a casual weed.
Distinguished by the four-rowed or six-rowed
flowering spike.

Wall Barley *Hordean murinum* Photographed 1 June

Photographed 1 June

Wall Barley *Hordeum murinum* L. Native
annual, common in lowland Britain on waste-
ground, roadsides and cultivated ground,
especially on disturbed soil. Children use the
flowerheads for darts which cling to clothes.
Height from 6 to 60cm. Flowers May to August.
Meadow Barley *H. secalinum* Schreb. is
common on meadows and pastures in the
south. Flowerheads are shorter and narrower.

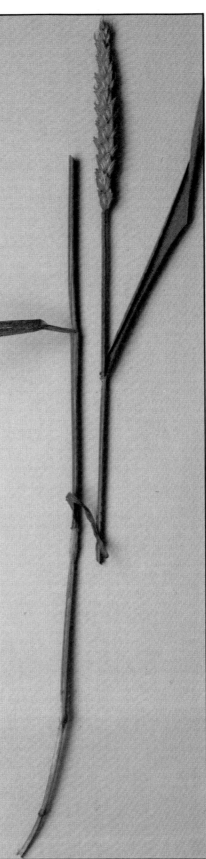

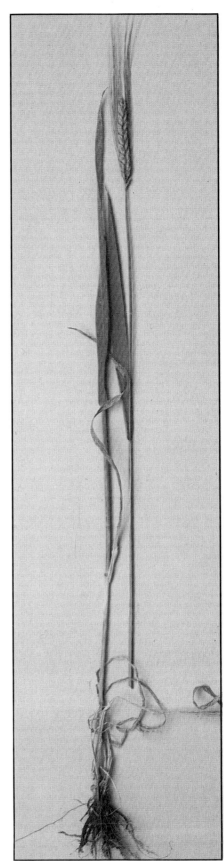

Photographed 12 July

Photographed 12 July

Photographed 12 July

Rye *Secale cereale* L. Introduced annual, cultivated in fields for food and livestock. Also used in eastern Europe to make rye bread and for brewing and the stems for thatching. Sometimes found as an escape from cultivation.

Bread Wheat *Triticum aestivum* L. The most commonly cultivated cereal crop with many different varieties and forms. The spike is four-sided and dense, each spikelet with several flowers. Mainly grown for human consumption, but also provides livestock fodder, and the straw can be used for thatching and matting.

Rivet Wheat or **Cone Wheat** *Triticum turgidum* L. Annual cultivated cereal, most commonly grown around the Mediterranean and southern Europe, and occasionally in Britain. It has a dense head, and each flower has a very long awn. Height to about 120cm. Flowers June to August.

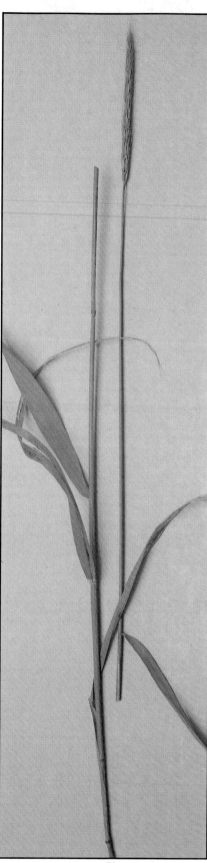

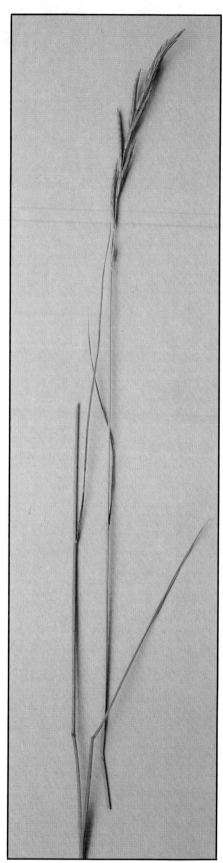

Photographed 19 June

Photographed 26 June

Photographed 28 June

Lyme-grass *Elymus arenarius* L. Native perennial, common on sand-dunes where its tough rhizomes bind the loose sand. Usually found on the less stable dunes nearest the sea and often mixed with Marram Grass and often planted as part of dune reclamation programmes. Height from 60 to 200cm. Flowers June to August.

Wood Barley *Hordelymus europaeus* (L.) Harz. Native perennial, found in woods and other shady places, mostly on calcareous soil in England, rare elsewhere. Height from 40 to 120cm. Wood Barley does not spread well vegetatively, therefore is short-lived. The name *Hordelymus* reflects this species' similarities to both *Hordeum* and *Elymus*. Flowers June to July.

Chalk False-brome or **Tor Grass** *Brachypodium pinnatum* (L.) Beauv. Native perennial, with creeping rhizomes. Found on chalk and limestone grassland in the south. Height 35 to 120cm. Flowers June to August.
Wood False-brome *B. sylvaticum* (Huds.) Beauv. has broad leaves, hairy sheaths and grows in woodland. Height 35 to 90cm. Flowers July to August.

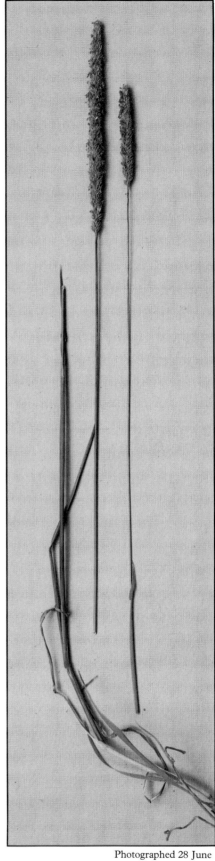

Photographed 19 June

Photographed 26 June

Photographed 28 June

Sand Cat's-tail or **Sand Timothy** *Phleum arenarium* L. Native annual of sand-dunes on most British coasts except on the north and west of Scotland. It forms small tufts and the stems rise from a curved or bent base. Height from 2 to 15cm. Flowers May to July.

Small Cat's-tail *Phleum bertolonii* DC. Native perennial with stolons, found in grassland and pasture on most types of soil, more common in England than elsewhere. Similar to Timothy Grass but generally smaller and less robust. It is an important forage grass. Height from 10 to 50cm. Flowers June to August.

Bohmer's Cat's-tail or **Purple-stem Cat's-tail** *Phleum phleoides* (L.) Karst. Native perennial, forming thick tufts. It grows only on dry sandy or chalk soils in south-east England. Similar to Timothy, but more slender and without the swollen stem base. Height from 10 to 70cm. Flowers June to August.

47

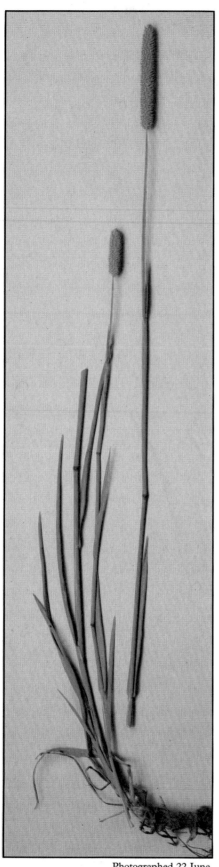

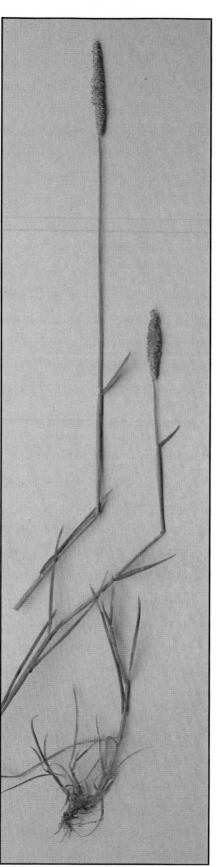

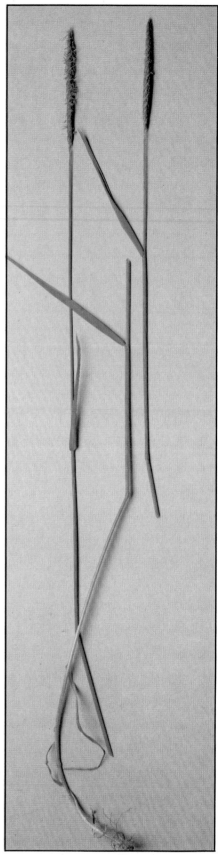

Photographed 22 June

Photographed 12 June

Photographed 1 June

Timothy Grass or **Cat's-tail** *Phleum pratense* L. Native perennial forming loose tufts. Common throughout Britain on pastures, roadsides and waste-ground. It forms an important fodder crop and is widely planted for both hay and grazing. It is named 'Timothy' after the man who introduced it to the United States in the eighteenth century. Height from 40 to 150cm. Flowers June to August.

Marsh Fox-tail or **Floating Fox-tail** *Alopecurus geniculatus* L. Native perennial, common on wet places, beside lakes and rivers throughout Britain. The stems have swollen nodes, are usually prostrate on the ground and sharply bent. Height from 15 to 45cm. Flowers June to July.

Slender Fox-tail or **Black Grass** *Alopecurus myosuroides* Huds. Native annual, found as a weed on waste and arable land, mainly in south-east England, scattered or rare elsewhere. Its seeds ripen before cereals so that if successive crops are grown on the same ground the weed increases in numbers from one year to the next. Height from 20 to 80cm. Flowers May to August.

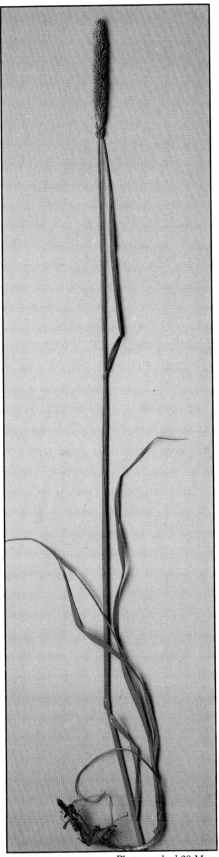

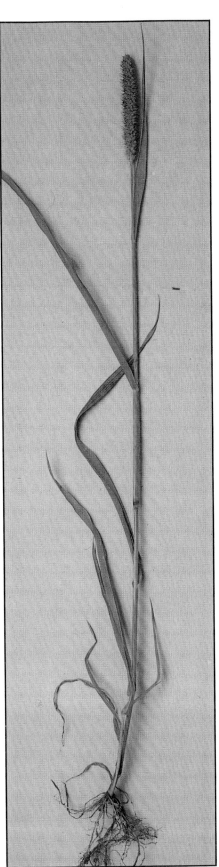

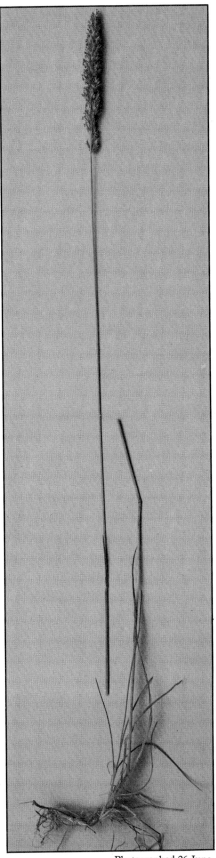

Photographed 30 May

Photographed 3 August

Photographed 26 June

Meadow Fox-tail or **Common Fox-tail**
Alopecurus pratensis L. Native perennial,
common throughout Britain on damp meadows
and grassland. It makes good grazing,
particularly early in the year. Many cultivated
forms have been introduced, so that the species
may appear to be extremely variable. Height
from 30 to 90cm. Flowers April to June.

Yellow Bristle-grass *Setaria lutescens* (Weig.)
Hubbard, synonym *S. glauca* auct. Introduced
annual, occasionally found as a weed of
cultivated or waste-ground. The ligule is a ring
of hairs. Height from 6 to 75cm. Flowers July
to October.
Rough Bristle-grass *S. verticillata* (L.)
Beauv. is also introduced. Flowerheads are
larger and broken into sections.

Crested Hair-grass *Koeleria cristata* (L.)
Pers. Native perennial, common on dry
calcareous grassland throughout Britain. It
forms dense tufts and has thin tough rhizomes.
Height from 10 to 60cm. Flowers June to July.
Somerset Grass *K. vallesiana* (Honck.)
Bertol. looks similar but has matted remains of
old leaves at the base of its thickened stems.
Only found on limestone hills in Somerset.

Marram Grass *Ammophila arenaria* Photographed 4 July

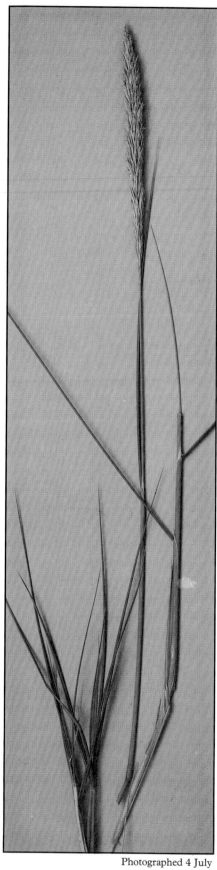

Photographed 4 July

Marram Grass *Ammophila arenaria* (L.)
Link. Native perennial, common and usually
dominant on sand dunes around British coasts.
Height 60 to 120cm. Rhizomes root at the
nodes, creeping along the loose sand and
binding it. Marram is often planted to stabilize
dunes. The leaves are rolled inwards, enclosing
a blue, ridged surface with a smooth, shiny
outer surface. Flowers July to August.

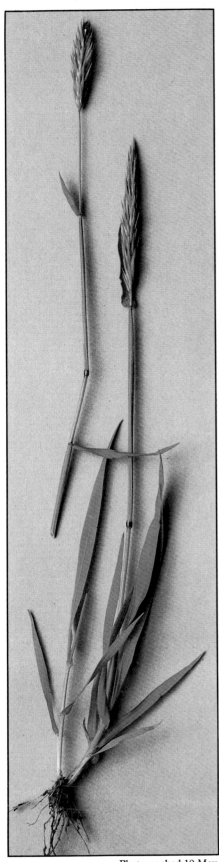

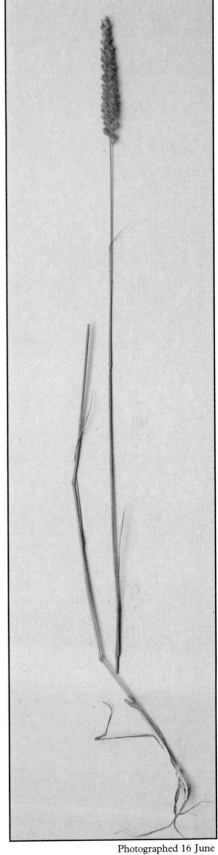

Photographed 10 May

Photographed 10 May

Photographed 16 June

Sweet Vernal-grass *Anthoxanthum odoratum* L. Native perennial, common on grassland on all types of soil especially on hill pastures and heaths. Sweet Vernal-grass has a strong hay scent when crushed or cut and is one of the earliest grasses to flower. Height from 30 to 100cm. Flowers April to July.

Blue Moor-grass or **Blue Sesleria** *Sesleria albicans* Kit, ex Schult., synonym *S. caerulea* (L.) Ard. subspecies *calcarea* (Celak.) Hegi. Native perennial frequent on limestone grassland in north England and Ireland and on mica-schist in Scotland, growing on pasture, rock-ledges and cliffs. Height from 10 to 45cm. Flowers April to June.

Crested Dog's-tail *Cynosurus cristatus* L. Native perennial forming tight clumps. It is found throughout Britain on grassland of all types. It produces an abundance of leaves and is drought-resistant, therefore useful for seeding permanent hill pastures for sheep grazing. Height from 5 to 80cm. Flowers June to August.

Photographed 7 June

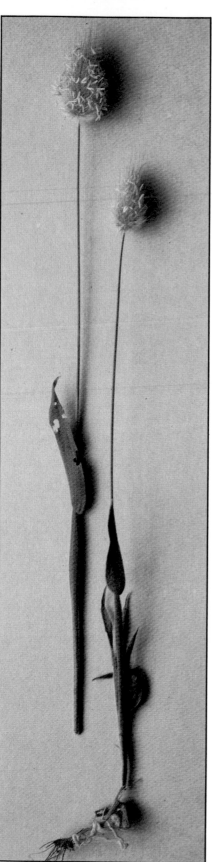

Photographed 7 June

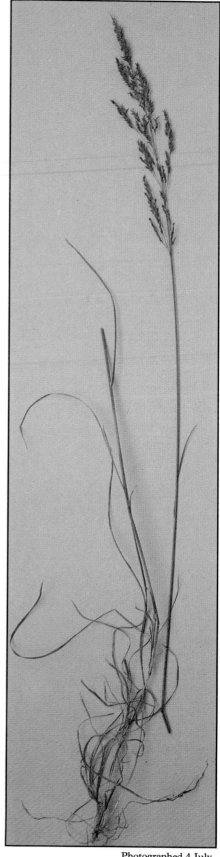

Photographed 4 July

Rough Dog's-tail *Cynosurus echinatus* L.
Introduced annual, native to the Mediterranean
region, occasionally found as a weed of
cultivated and waste-ground and sometimes
grown as a decorative grass for flower
arrangement. Like the Crested Dog's-tail the
spikelets are arranged on one side only of the
spike but are broader with long awns. Height
from 10 to 100cm. Flowers June to July.

Hare's-tail *Lagurus ovatus* L. Introduced
annual, native to the Mediterranean region,
naturalized in the Channel Isles and
occasionally found in the south of England on
rubbish tips or waste-ground. Often cultivated
in gardens, dried and dyed bright colours for
winter decoration. Height from 5 to 60cm.
Flowers June to August.

Velvet Bent *Agrostis canina* L. subspecies
canina. Native perennial forming tufts with
creeping stolons. Common throughout Britain
in wet places in meadows, ditches, heaths and
pondsides. The flowering stems are often
decumbent and the leaves are narrow and flat.
Height from 15 to 75cm. Flowers June to July.

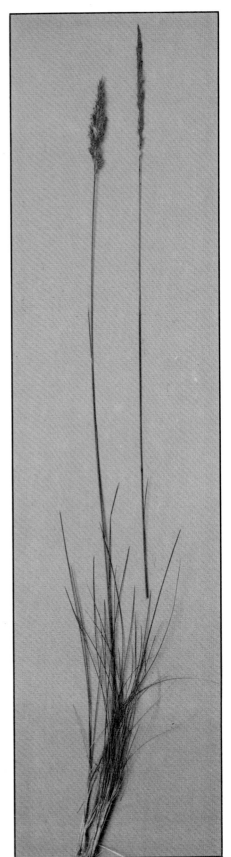

Photographed 10 July

Photographed 26 June

Photographed 29 June

Common Bent-grass, Black Bent or **Red Top** *Agrostis gigantea* Roth. Native perennial, found in open woods, grassy banks and as a weed of arable land, most common in south England. In North America it has been introduced and grown for hay and to bind the soil with its tough rhizomes. Height from 40 to 120cm. *A. gigantea* has longer ligules than *A. tenuis*. Flowers June to August.

Water Bent *Agrostis semiverticillata* (Forsk.) C. Christ. Introduced perennial or annual, native to the Mediterranean region, occasionally found on rubbish tips and waste-ground. The flower spike is much more dense in appearance than other *Agrostis* species. Height from 10 to 60cm. Flowers June to August.

Bristle-leaved Bent *Agrostis setacea* Curt. Native perennial, which forms dense tufts, found only in south and south-west England and south Wales where it may be common on sandy and peaty moors and heaths. Height from 10 to 60cm. Flowers June to July.

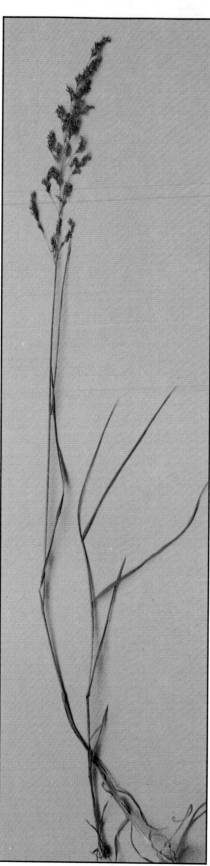

Photographed 10 July

Photographed 26 June

Photographed 3 July

Fiorin or **Creeping Bent** *Agrostis stolonifera* L. Native perennial, common on grassland and waste-ground throughout Britain. Differs from most other *Agrostis* species by having stolons, rather than rhizomes, as shown by its procumbent stem base which roots at the nodes. Height from 8 to 40cm. Flowers July to August.

Common Bent or **Brown Top** *Agrostis tenuis* Sibth. Native perennial, very common and found throughout Britain on grassland, moors, waste-ground, usually on poor acid soils on mountains and moorland. It is used as a lawn grass for putting or bowling greens where it forms a fine turf, and mixed with other grasses for lawns in gardens. Height from 10 to 70cm. Flowers June to August.

Reed-grass or **Reed Canary-grass** *Phalaris arundinacea* L. Native perennial, found throughout Britain by rivers, lakes, in marshes and wet meadows. Its rhizomes spread over a wide area and produce tall plants from 60 to 120cm. Sometimes grown for grazing on wet ground. The flowerhead opens wide when mature. Flowers June to July.

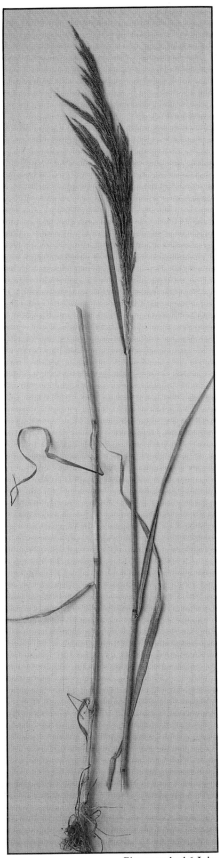

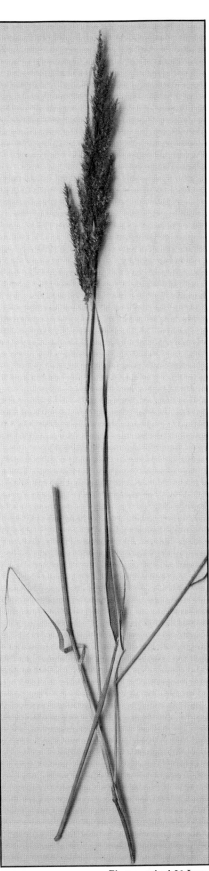

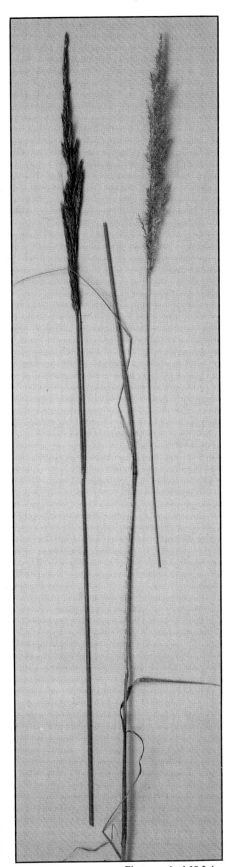

Photographed 6 July

Photographed 26 June

Photographed 25 July

Loose Silky-bent or **Wind Grass** *Apera spica-venti* (L.) Beauv. Annual, mainly found in dry arable or waste land in the south and east. Thought to have been introduced to Britain a long time ago and now well established. It can be a troublesome weed but it is so attractive that it is grown in gardens and used for flower arrangement. Height from 30 to 100cm. Flowers June to August.

Purple Small-reed *Calamagrostis canescens* (Weber) Roth. Native perennial, forming large loose tufts in fens, marshes and wet woods. Found most frequently in the south and east. Leaves are rough on both surfaces. Height 60 to 120cm. Flowers June to July.
Narrow Small-reed *C. stricta* (Timm) Koeler is rare, found in a few marshes and bogs. It is smaller, 40 to 100cm, and narrower.

Bush Grass or **Small-reed** *Calamagrostis epigejos* (L.) Roth. Native perennial, forming thick clumps in wet woodland, scrub and fens. Most frequent on heavy soils in England. Sometimes planted by lakes or ponds in gardens and estates. The leaves are hairless on the upper surface, distinguishing it from the Purple Small-reed. Height from 60 to 200cm. Flowers June to August.

Photographed 10 May

Photographed 22 May

Photographed 22 May

Wood Millet *Milium effusum* L. Native perennial forming loose tufts. Fairly common in England in deciduous woods and damp heavy soils, rarer in Scotland, Ireland and Wales. Wood Millet has been sown in woodland on estates for ornament and as food for game birds. Height from 45 to 180cm. Flowers May to July.

Wood Melick *Melica uniflora* Retz. Native perennial, with creeping rhizomes forming loose, leafy patches. Common in woods and shady places throughout Britain, though rare in the north of Scotland and Ireland. Each spikelet contains only one flower. Height from 20 to 60cm. Flowers May to July.

Mountain Melick or **Nodding Melick** *Melica nutans* L. Native perennial, found in woods and wood edges, often on limestone, more frequent in Scotland, north and west England and Wales, but rather uncommon. Height from 20 to 60cm. Flowers May to July.

Tufted Hair-grass or **Tussock-grass** *Deschampsia caespitosa* Photographed 21 June

Photographed 21 June

Tufted Hair-grass or **Tussock-grass**
Deschampsia caespitosa (L.) Beauv. Native
perennial, which grows into a distinctively large
tuft or tussock. Found on wet soils on
moorland, damp meadows and ditches
throughout Britain. Height from 20 to 200cm.
The leaves are tough with an extremely rough
upper surface which can cause nasty cuts.
Flowers June to August.

Wavy Hair-grass *Deschampsia flexuosa* Photographed 9 June

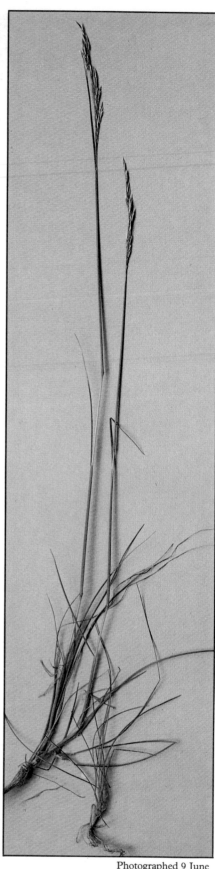

Photographed 9 June

Wavy Hair-grass *Deschampsia flexuosa* (L.)
Trin. Native tuft-forming perennial, sometimes
spreading by rhizomes. Found throughout
Britain on sandy or peaty soils, often common
on moorland or clearings in woodland, the
delicate heads appearing like a pink mist on
the ground. The flowerhead branches are
strongly wavy. Height from 50 to 200cm.
Flowers June to July.

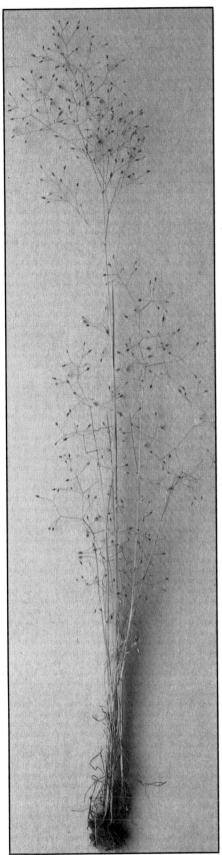

Photographed 12 June

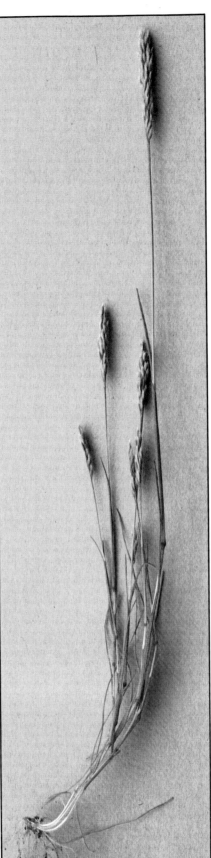

Photographed 31 May

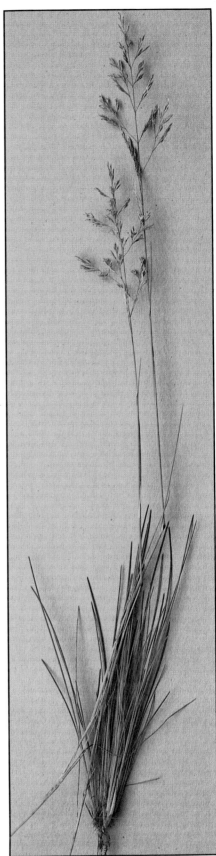

Photographed 28 June

Silvery Hair-grass *Aira caryophyllea* L. Native annual, found throughout Britain on dry, sandy soils and walls. It is one of our most attractive grasses and has been recommended for planting in rockeries. Height from 10 to 30cm. Flowers May to July.

Early Hair-grass *Aira praecox* L. Native annual, common throughout Britain on dry sandy soils, walls and sand dunes. It is one of the first grasses to flower and quickly dries out in early summer. Height from 5 to 20cm. Flowers March to June.

Grey Hair-grass *Corynephorus canescens* (L.) Beauv. Native perennial which is rare and found only on some sand dunes on the coast of East Anglia, the Channel Isles and the east coast of Scotland. Its spikelets bear awns which are club shaped (as seen under a hand lens). This is completely distinctive and is referred to in its name which in Greek means club-bearing. Height from 10 to 35cm. Flowers June to July.

Yorkshire Fog *Holcus lanatus* Photographed 12 June

Photographed 12 June

Yorkshire Fog *Holcus lanatus* L. Native
perennial, common throughout Britain on
pasture, roadsides, waste-ground, open
woodland on all types of soil. It is covered
with soft hairs which give the plant a soft
velvety feel. Often flushed pink or purple or
may be almost white. Height from 20 to
100cm. Flowers May to August.

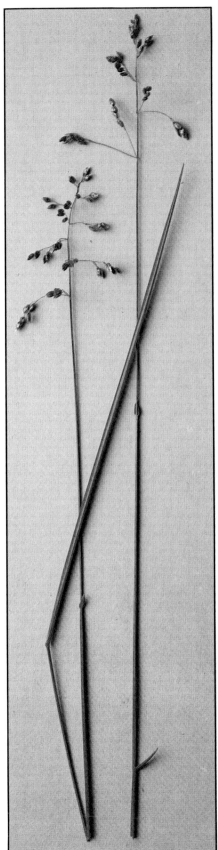

Photographed 4 July

Photographed 3 August

Photographed 22 May

Creeping Soft Grass *Holcus mollis* L. Native perennial, found throughout Britain on acid soils and may be a bad weed of sandy arable land. Less common than Yorkshire Fog which it closely resembles. Easily distinguished by the presence of rhizomes and the long hairs around each node which have earned it the nickname 'Hairy-knees'. Height from 20 to 100cm. Flowers June to August.

Purple Moor-grass *Molinia caerulea* (L.) Moench. Native perennial forming tufts or tussocks. Common and often dominant on damp moors, heaths and fens throughout Britain. The flowerhead is usually dark purple, but may be pinkish, yellowish or green. Height from 15 to 120cm. Flowers July to September.

Holy Grass *Hierochloë odorata* (L.) Beauv. Native perennial, very rare, found wild in only a few damp grassy habitats in Scotland and Ireland. It is sweetly aromatic and named 'Vanilla Grass' in North America. In central Europe it was dedicated to the Virgin Mary and laid at church doors for festival days. Height from 20 to 50cm. Flowers late March to May.

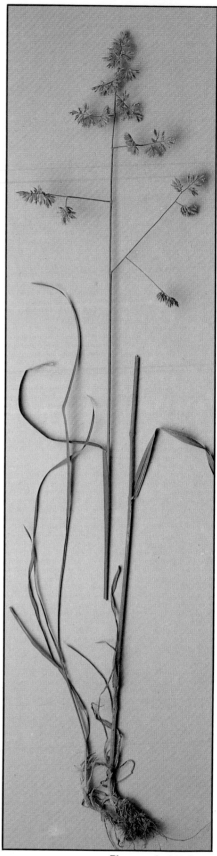

Photographed 7 June

Photographed 12 June

Photographed 19 June

Common Quaking-grass or **Totter Grass**
Briza media L. Native perennial, found
throughout Britain on most types of grassland
though most common on the calcareous ground
of south England. It has little value for grazing
as it produces very few leaves. Height from
20 to 75cm. One of our most attractive grasses,
the flowerheads are often dried for winter
flower arrangement. Flowers June to August.

Small Quaking-grass *Briza minor* L.
Native annual, found on waste and cultivated
ground and road-sides in south-west England.
Sometimes grown in gardens for ornament and
found on rubbish tips as a garden escape.
Height from 10 to 60cm. Flowers June to
September.

Cocksfoot *Dactylis glomerata* L. Native
perennial, common throughout Britain on
grassland, meadows, roadsides and waste-
ground. This grass has long been used for
grazing and haymaking and several strains can
be found. Height from 20 to 140cm. Flowers
June to September.

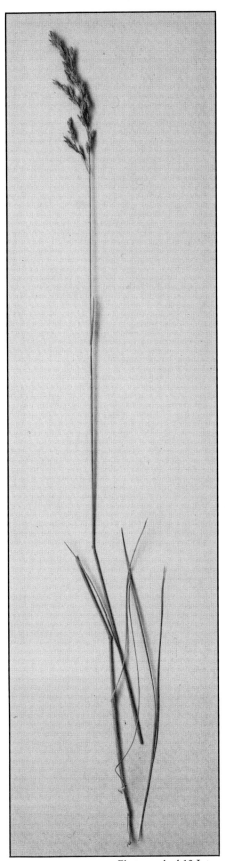

Photographed 12 June

Photographed 10 May

Photographed 10 May

Narrow-leaved Meadow-grass *Poa angustifolia* L. Native perennial, spreading by rhizomes. Found on hill grassland particularly on chalk, limestone or sandy soils, most common in the south of England. Similar to Smooth Meadow-grass but is smaller and has narrower leaves. Height from 20 to 60cm. Flowers April to June.

Annual Meadow-grass *Poa annua* L. Native annual, common throughout Britain on waste-ground, roadsides, fields, gardens and even cracks in pavements. It is often found in lawns where it continuously re-seeds itself. Height from 3 to 30cm. Flowers all year.

Bulbous Meadow-grass *Poa bulbosa* L. Native perennial, rare and found only on sandy ground in the south and east of England. It is easily recognized by the bulbous stem bases clustered together in a thick tuft. These bulbs persist after the plant dies back and each may produce a new plant the following season. Height from 5 to 40cm. Flowers March to May.

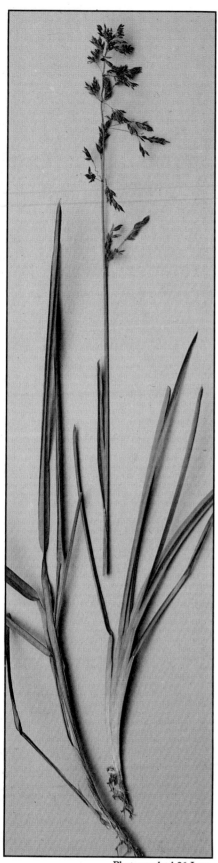

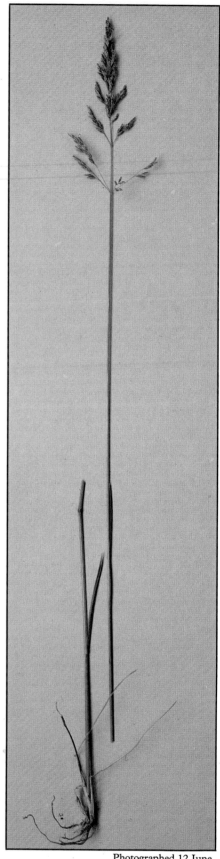

Photographed 26 June

Photographed 12 June

Photographed 12 June

Broad-leaved Meadow-grass or **Chaix's Meadow-grass** *Poa chaixii* Vill. Introduced perennial, once planted in woodland as an ornamental, now naturalized in open woodland and wood edges in parts of Scotland, England and Wales. Larger than most other Meadow-grasses with broader leaves and thicker tufts. Height from 60 to 120cm. Flowers May to July.

Wood Meadow-grass *Poa nemoralis* L. Native perennial, found throughout Britain forming loose tufts in woods, hedgerows and other shady places. It has a more delicate, slender appearance than other Meadow-grasses and has been planted in woodland as an ornamental. Height from 15 to 90cm. Flowers June to July.

Smooth Meadow-grass *Poa pratensis* L. Native perennial with creeping rhizomes, common throughout Britain on pasture, arable land, roadsides, waste-ground and walls. It is used for hay, grazing and on park and sportsground lawns. Height from 10 to 90cm. Flowers May to early July.

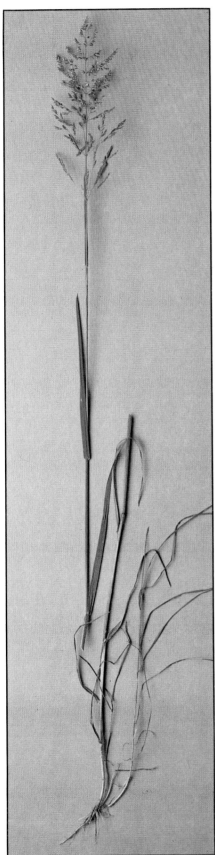

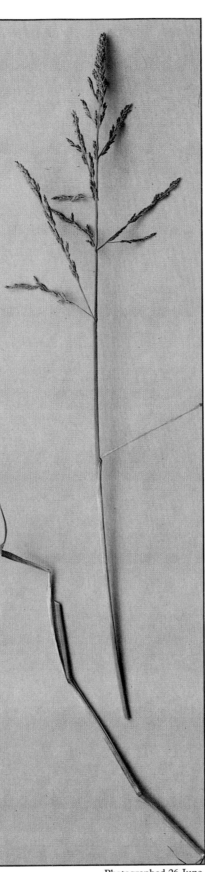

Photographed 5 June

Photographed 26 June

Photographed 30 May

Rough Meadow-grass *Poa trivialis* L. Native perennial with creeping stolons, common throughout Britain in meadows, pastures and waste places. It is easily distinguished from other Meadow-grasses by its rough leaf-sheaths and long pointed ligules. Useful for grazing on heavy and damp soils and sometimes used in lawns on similar soil. Height from 20 to 100cm. Flowers June to July.

Borrer's Salt-marsh Grass *Puccinellia fasciculata* (Torr.) Bicknell. Native perennial, rather rare growing only on salt marshes and muddy ground near the sea in the south of England, Wales and Ireland. It forms a round spreading tuft. Height from 6 to 60cm. Flowers June to September.

Fern Grass or **Hard Poa** *Catapodium rigidum* (L.) C.E. Hubbard. Native annual, found on dry sandy or rocky ground, walls and banks usually on calcareous soil. Most common in the south. It forms a stiff, hard tuft. Height from 2 to 30cm. Flowers May to July.
Stiff Sand-grass *C. marinum* (L.) C.E. Hubbard is similar with broader leaves. Found on dunes and shingle.

Photographed 26 June

Photographed 25 July

Photographed 25 July

Glaucous Sweet-grass *Glyceria declinata*
Breb. Native tufted perennial. Stems rise from
a curved or bent base. Found on wet ground at
the edges of ponds, rivers or streams, less
common in the north. Height from 10 to 45cm.
Flowers June to September.
Plicate Sweet-grass *Glyceria plicata* Fries is
frequent in similar habitats, has larger, more
branched flowerheads and hairy leaf-sheaths.

Floating Sweet-grass or **Flote-grass**
Glyceria fluitans (L.) R. Br. Native perennial,
aquatic, growing in shallow water at lake and
streamsides and ditches, often in abundance.
Found throughout Britain and its succulent
foliage is much loved by cattle. Height from
60 to 100cm, usually prostrate and floating.
Flowers May to August.

Reed Sweet-grass *Glyceria maxima* (Hartm.)
Holmb. Native perennial, common in the
lowlands of England on wet ground, in lakes
and rivers and on canal banks. It spreads by
thick rhizomes and may grow in fairly deep
water. Height from 90 to 125cm. Flowers
June to August.

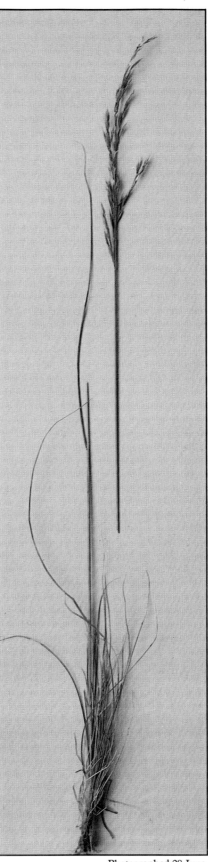

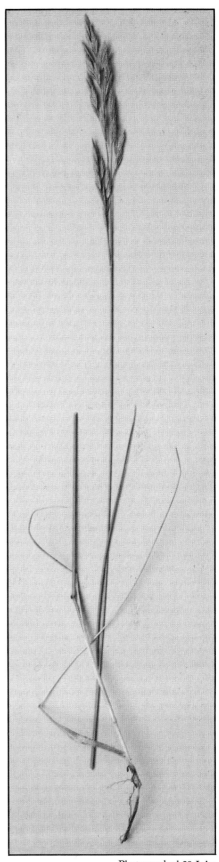

Photographed 26 July

Photographed 28 June

Photographed 29 July

Tall Fescue *Festuca arundinacea* Schreb.
Native perennial, found throughout Britain
in grassy places and banks on most types of
soil. It forms thick tufts. The auricles have a
row of short hairs. Height from 50 to 200cm.
Flowers June to August.
Meadow Fescue *F. pratensis* Huds. is
common in meadows and grassland in England,
it has larger spikelets and hairless auricles.

Various-leaved Fescue *Festuca heterophylla*
Lam. Tufted perennial, thought to have been
introduced for fodder early last century. Rare,
but naturalized in woods and dry gravelly or
sandy banks in parts of south England.
Leaves on the stem are flat, about 2 to 4mm
wide, while the basal leaves are narrow and
bristle-like. Height from 60 to 120cm. Flowers
June to July.

Rush-leaved Fescue *Festuca juncifolia*
St.-Amans. Native perennial with far-reaching
rhizomes. Uncommon, found on sand dunes of
south and east coasts. Height from 20 to 90cm.
It is bluish-green and has distinctive stiff,
narrow pungent leaves. Flowers July to August.
Giant Fescue *F. gigantea* (L.) Vill. is common
in damp woods. Distinguished by its awns and
large size. Height 45 to 150cm.

Creeping Fescue or **Red Fescue** *Festuca rubra* subsp. *rubra* Photographed 9 June

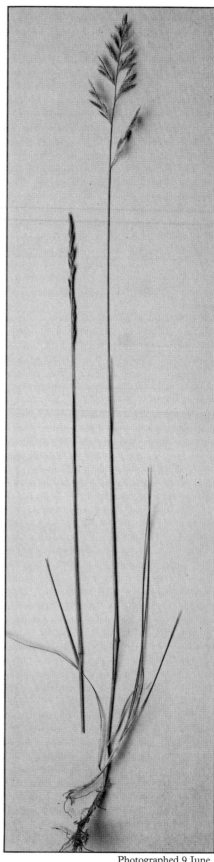

Photographed 9 June

Creeping Fescue or **Red Fescue** *Festuca rubra* L. subspecies *rubra*. Native perennial with long rhizomes, common throughout Britain on sand dunes, salt marshes, lowland meadows and hill grassland. The flowerheads are stouter than Sheep's Fescue and are usually pinkish or purplish. Height from about 20 to 90cm. Flowers May to July.

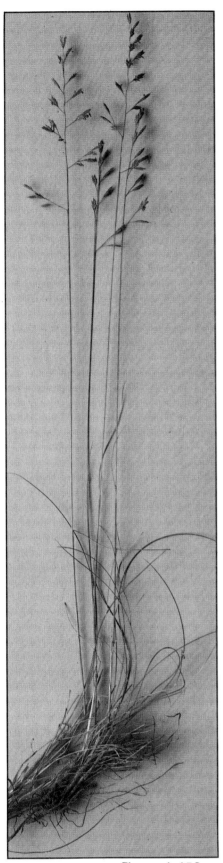

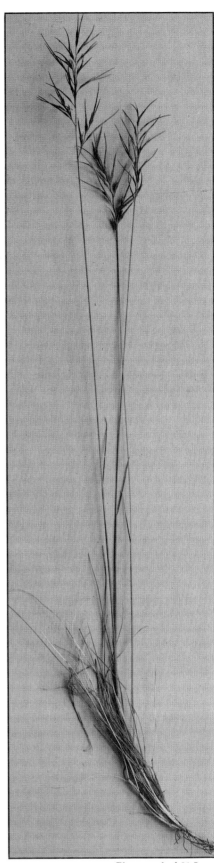

Photographed 7 June

Photographed 12 June

Photographed 21 June

Sheep's Fescue *Festuca ovina* L. Native perennial which forms thick tufts. Common throughout Britain on poor soils particularly on hills or moorland. It is often abundant on hill pastures where it is a valuable part of the diet of sheep. Height from 5 to 60cm. Flowers May to July.

Fine-leaved Sheep's Fescue *Festuca tenuifolia* Sibth. Native perennial, very similar to Sheep's Fescue but does not have awns. Found throughout Britain on heaths, moorland and hill grassland on acid or peaty soils. Often used as a lawn grass as its fine leaves form a dense sward which can be closely mown. Height from 10 to 45cm. Flowers May to June.

Viviparous Fescue *Festuca vivipara* (L.) Sm. Native perennial, which grows on hill pasture and moorland in the north and west. It is similar in appearance to Sheep's Fescue except that the spikelets do not produce seed but tiny plantlets, which fall on the ground and develop into new plants. Height from 5 to 60cm. Flowers May to July.

Photographed 26 June

Photographed 12 July

Photographed 24 May

Lesser Hairy Brome *Bromus benekenii* (Lange) Trimen, synonym *Zerna benekenii* (Lange) Lindm. Native tufted perennial, in woodland and hedgerows usually on chalk or limestone soil, rare and found in a few places throughout England, Wales and south Scotland. Uppermost leaf-sheaths are hairless. Height from 60 to 90cm. Flowers June to August.

California Brome *Bromus carinatus* Hook. & Arn., synonym *Ceratochloa carinata* (Hook. & Arn.) Tutin. Introduced perennial, originally from North America, now naturalized in parts of England, notably by the River Thames at Kew and Oxford. Height from 60 to 80cm. Flowers June to August.

Great Brome *Bromus diandrus* Roth, synonym *Anisantha diandra* (Roth) Tutin. Annual, native to the Mediterranean region, naturalized on sandy shores in the Channel Isles and a few places in the south of England. Great Brome is rather stout and softly hairy. Height from 40 to 80cm. Flowers May to July.

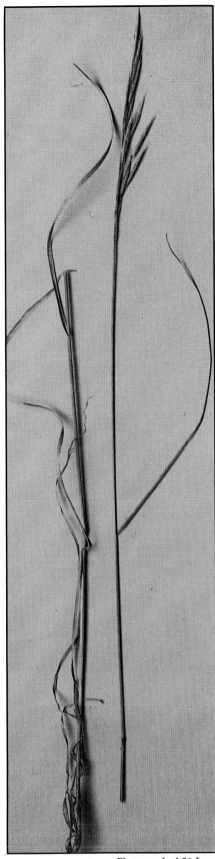

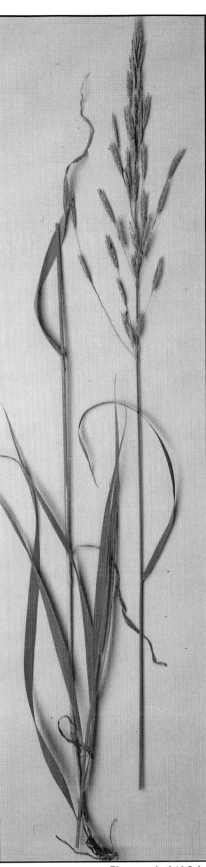

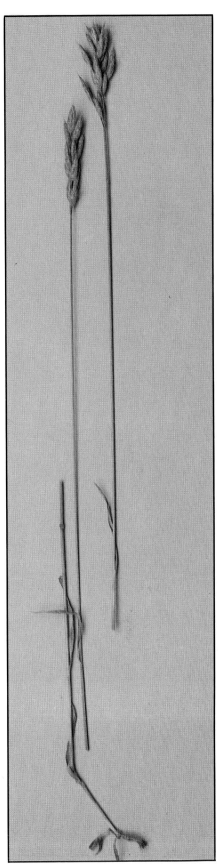

Photographed 26 June

Photographed 12 July

Photographed 31 May

Upright Brome *Bromus erectus* Huds.,
synonym *Zerna erecta* (Huds.) S.F. Gray.
Native perennial, found on dry calcareous soils
in the south and east of England, rare
elsewhere. The tall, stout culms often turn red
or purplish through the summer. Height from
50 to 120cm. Flowers June to July.

Hungarian Brome *Bromus inermis* Leyss.,
synonym *Zerna inermis* (Leyss.) Lindm.
Introduced perennial, native to central Europe
and Asia, once cultivated for fodder, and now
naturalized on dry sandy or stony ground in a
few places in England. Spreads by means of
rhizomes which distinguish this grass from
Upright Brome. Height from 50 to 150cm.
Flowers June to July.

Lop-grass or **Soft Brome** *Bromus mollis* L.
Native annual or biennial, common on waste-
ground, fields, sand dunes and roadsides. The
whole plant is softly hairy. Height from 25 to
100cm. Flowers May to July.
Slender Brome *B. lepidus* Holmb. is similar
but has smaller, usually hairless spikelets.
Frequent in cultivated grassland. Height
10 to 90cm. Flowers May to July.

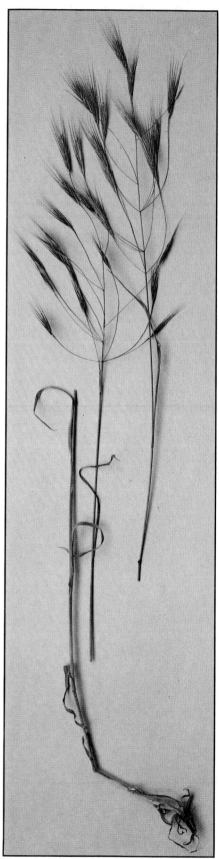

Photographed 27 July

Photographed 10 July

Photographed 30 May

Hairy Brome or **Wood Brome** *Bromus ramosus* Huds. Native and common, found in woods and shady places throughout Britain, though rare in Scotland. It has stiff open flowerheads and long broad leaves with hairy upper sheaths. Height is 45 to 190cm. Flowers July to August.

Rye Brome *Bromus secalinus* L. Introduced annual or biennial, found as a weed of arable land. Uncommon, found scattered through England. Height from 20 to 120cm. Flowers June to July.

Meadow Brome *Bromus commutatus* Schrad. is similar with larger spikelets and more hairy leaf-sheaths. It grows in meadows and waste-ground. Height from 40 to 120cm.

Barren Brome *Bromus sterilis* L., synonym *Anisantha sterilis* (L.) Nevski. Native annual or biennial, common on waste and cultivated ground, hedgerows, and roadsides in lowland Britain. The culm may be erect or drooping and may be green or purple. Height from 20 to 100cm. Flowers May to July.

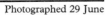

Photographed 29 June

Photographed 12 June

Photographed 5 September

Bearded Fescue *Vulpia ambigua* (Le Gall)
A.G. More. Native annual; rare, found on
sandy heaths and near the sea in the south and
east. Height 5 to 30cm. Flowers May to June.
Rat's-tail Fescue *Vulpia myuros* (L.)
C.C. Gmel. is taller with larger, slightly
drooping flowerheads. Common on waste-
ground and dry grassland in the south and
west. Height from 10 to 70cm.

Squirrel-tail Fescue *Vulpia bromoides* (L.)
S.F. Gray. Native annual, found on dry soils
on heaths, hills, roadsides and waste-ground.
Most common in the south and east of England
and Ireland, scattered elsewhere. Height from
5 to 60cm. Flowers May to July.

Common Reed *Phragmites australis* (Cav.)
Trin. ex Steud., synonym *P. communis* Trin.
Native perennial with thick rhizomes and
stolons. Common in marshes, fens and shallow
water growing over large areas. The tough
stems and leaves are used for thatching and
matting and the flowerheads are most
decorative when dried. Height from 150 to
300cm. Flowers late August to October.

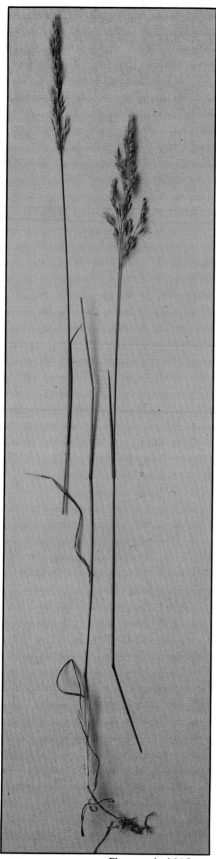

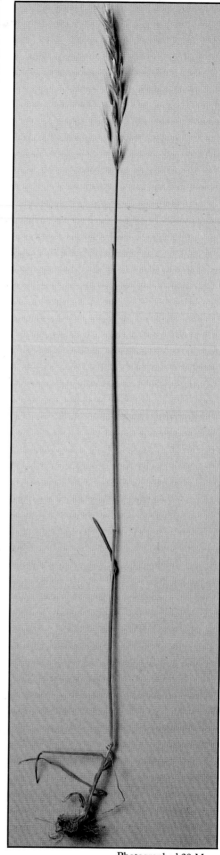

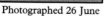

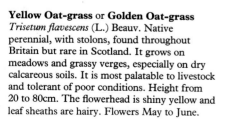

Photographed 26 June

Photographed 9 June

Photographed 30 May

Yellow Oat-grass or **Golden Oat-grass**
Trisetum flavescens (L.) Beauv. Native
perennial, with stolons, found throughout
Britain but rare in Scotland. It grows on
meadows and grassy verges, especially on dry
calcareous soils. It is most palatable to livestock
and tolerant of poor conditions. Height from
20 to 80cm. The flowerhead is shiny yellow and
leaf sheaths are hairy. Flowers May to June.

Meadow Oat-grass *Helictotrichon pratense*
(L.) Pilger. Native perennial, found on chalk or
limestone grassland. It is hairless, forms dense
short tufts and may be common on chalk
downs. Height from 30 to 80cm. Flowers
June to July.

Hairy Oat-grass *Helictotrichon pubescens*
(Huds.) Pilger. Native perennial forming loose
tufts. It is taller than the Meadow Oat-grass
and has softer, hairy sheaths and leaves.
Common on damp lowland soils throughout
England and the west of Scotland. Height from
30 to 100cm. Flowers May to July.

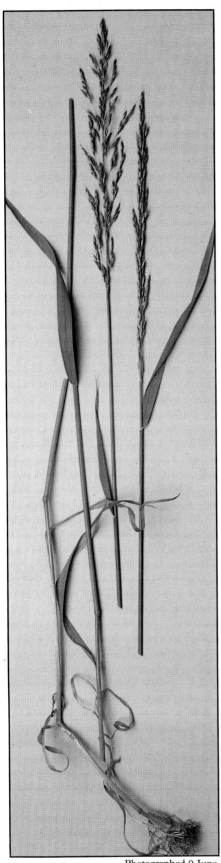

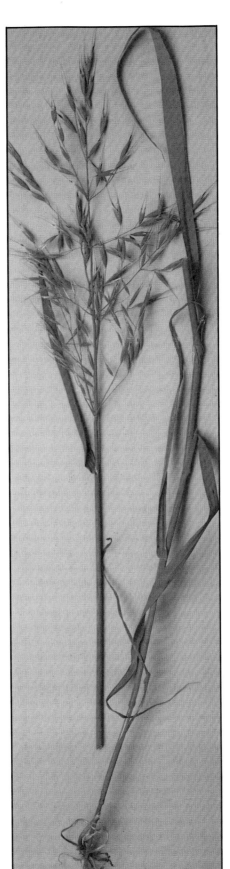

Photographed 9 June

Photographed 11 July

Photographed 11 July

False Oat-grass *Arrhenatherum elatius* (L.) Beauv. ex J. & C. Presl. Native perennial, tufted and deep-rooting, common on roadsides, grassy banks and rough grassland throughout Britain. Useful for hay as it is very leafy and drought-resistant. Height from 50 to 150cm. Flowers June to September.

Wild Oat *Avena fatua* L. Introduced annual, now naturalized on arable land among crops and on waste-ground, particularly in south and east England. Height from 30 to 150cm. Easily distinguished by the spreading clusters of flowers or spikelets which bear long blackish awns. Flowers June to September.

Winter Wild Oat *Avena ludoviciana* Durieu. Annual, possibly introduced from France among wheat seed during the First World War. Now a weed of arable land in the south of England. The spikelets fall in half when ripe. Height 60 to 180cm. Flowers July to August.
Cultivated Oat *A. sativa* L. is sometimes found as a weed. Smaller with shorter awns. Height from 50 to 120cm.

Lady Fern *Athyrium filix-femina* Photographed 24 July

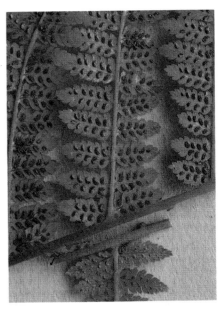

Lady Fern *Athyrium filix-femina* (L.) Roth. Native, forming a dense clump with short rhizomes. Common throughout Britain in damp woods, hedgerows, rocks and marshes but generally avoiding calcareous soils. An extremely variable fern but usually has doubly-pinnate fronds (left) about 20 to 100cm long with a scaly stem about one quarter to one half the length of the whole. Its delicate texture and graceful feathery appearance has earned it the name Lady Fern. The narrow sori (above), often hooked into a 'comma' shape, in two rows on the underside of each segment are a good distinguishing feature. Spores ripe July to August.

Photographed July

Alpine Lady Fern *Athyrium distentifolium* Tausch ex Opiz, synonym *A. alpestre* (Hoppe) Rylands, non Clairv. Native, uncommon and found on rocks and scree on high mountains in the Scottish highlands (photograph above). Similar to Lady Fern but smaller and with circular sori. Spores ripe July to August.

Lady Fern *Athyrium filix-femina*

Male Fern *Dryopteris filix-mas*

Photographed 22 September

Male Fern *Dryopteris filix-mas* (L.) Schott.
Native, forming large clumps with thick
rhizomes. Probably the most common British
fern, found in damp woods, hedgerows and
other shady places throughout the country.
The fronds (left) are usually 40 to 90cm in
length with sparse pale scales on their stems.
The sori (top) are large and circular, covered
by a kidney-shaped flap, and number between
five and six on each side of the largest leaf
divisions. Many old beliefs about the power of
fern spores to confer invisibility to the carrier
probably relate to Male Fern. Its roots were
dug up on St John's Eve, carved into the shape
of a hand and baked to make a charm to ward
off witches and evil spirits. Spores ripe July to
August.

Male Fern *Dryopteris filix-mas*

Scaly Male Fern *Dryopteris pseudomas*

Photographed 21 June

Scaly Male Fern *Dryopteris pseudomas*
(Woll.) Holub & Pouzar, synonym *D. borreri*
auct. Native, found throughout Britain in
woods and on scree, usually on acid soil.
Similar to Male Fern but the stem is densely
covered with bright orange scales and the
unfurling leaves in spring are yellowish-green.
The smallest leaf divisions are toothed only at
the tips, not on the sides as in Male Fern.
Spores ripe July to October.

Scaly Male Fern *Dryopteris pseudomas*

Dwarf Male Fern or **Mountain Male Fern**
Dryopteris oreades

Photographed 19 July

Dwarf Male Fern or **Mountain Male Fern**
Dryopteris oreades Fomin, synonym
D. abbreviata auct. Native, found on rock
ledges, screes and dry stone walls in the
mountain districts of Britain often forming
thick clumps of many plants together. Fronds
(left) are up to about 50cm long with concave
pinnae, ie turning upwards at tips. The sori
(top) are also helpful in distinguishing the
Dwarf Male Fern as there are rarely more than
three under each leaf division, where there
are usually five or six on Male Fern. Spores
ripe July to September.

Dwarf Male Fern or **Mountain Male Fern** *Dryopteris oreades*

Crested Buckler Fern *Dryopteris cristata*

Photographed June

Crested Buckler Fern *Dryopteris cristata*
(L.) A. Gray. Native, rare and apparently
decreasing, found in bogs and wet heaths in
the south-east of England. Sterile fronds are up
to 45cm and spreading (left in photograph
left); fertile ones are up to about 100cm and
stand erect (right in photograph left). They are
narrow and the fertile leaflets are widely
spaced and twisted round into a horizontal
position like the rungs of a ladder. Spores ripe
July to August.

Crested Buckler Fern *Dryopteris cristata*

Rigid Buckler Fern *Dryopteris villarii*
subsp. *submontana*

Photographed 19 July

Rigid Buckler Fern *Dryopteris villarii*
(Bell.) Woynar ex Schinz & Thell. subsp.
submontana Fraser-Jenkins & Jermy, synonym
D. rigida (Swartz) A. Gray. Native, rare,
found only in cracks or crevices in limestone
rocks in north Wales and north-west England.
Fronds (left) are 20 to 60cm long with wiry
stems about half the length of the whole. They
have a mild aromatic fragrance and glands on
the surface give the leaves a grey appearance.
Sori (top) have kidney-shaped protective flaps.
Spores ripe July to August.

Rigid Buckler Fern *Dryopteris villarii* subsp. *submontana*

Narrow Buckler Fern *Dryopteris carthusiana*

Photographed 26 July

Narrow Buckler Fern *Dryopteris carthusiana*
(Vill.) H. P. Fuchs, synonyms *D. spinulosa*
Watt, *D. lanceolatocristata* (Hoffm.) Alston.
Native, found in damp woods or marshes
throughout Britain though rarely in profusion,
less common in east Scotland and Ireland. Very
similar to the Broad Buckler Fern but usually
smaller and narrower with uniformly pale-
coloured scales on the proportionately longer
stems. Leaves are 30 to 120cm long. Spores
ripe July to September.

Narrow Buckler Fern *Dryopteris carthusiana*

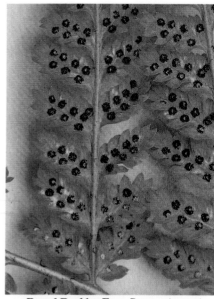

Broad Buckler Fern *Dryopteris austriaca*

Photographed 2 July

Broad Buckler Fern *Dryopteris austriaca*
(Jacq.) Woynar, synonym *D. dilatata* (Hoffm.)
A. Gray. Native, common in woods, hedgerows,
scrub and shady rock ledges throughout
Britain. Fronds (left) are broader and longer
than the Narrow Buckler Fern, more suddenly
narrowed towards the tip. Scales on the stem
have a dark brown streak in the centre, which
makes a good distinguishing feature. Spores
ripe July to September.

Broad Buckler Fern *Dryopteris austriaca*

Photographed September

Hay-scented Buckler Fern *Dryopteris aemula* (Ait.) Kuntze. Native, on shaded rocky places in woods and hedgebanks, most common in the west and south. Fronds (left) are 15 to 60cm long with concave segments, curled upwards at tips. The long dark-based stems are covered in reddish-brown scales. It has a scent of new mown hay when crushed. Sori are in two rows, nearer the centre of the segment than the edge. Spores ripe July to September.

Photographed June

Alpine Buckler Fern *Dryopteris expansa* (C. Presl.) Fraser-Jenkins & Jermy, synonym *D. assimilis* S. Walker. Native, found on rock crevices in mountain districts but distribution uncertain due to confusion with the Broad Buckler Fern. Fronds are smaller and paler, 7 to 60cm, stem scales may be light brown or with a dark brown stripe. Spores ripe July to September.

Hay-scented Buckler Fern *Dryopteris aemula*

Mountain Fern or **Lemon-scented Fern** *Oreopteris limbosperma* Photographed 22 June

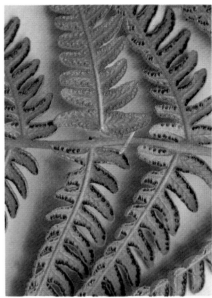

Mountain Fern or **Lemon-scented Fern**
Oreopteris limbosperma

Mountain Fern or **Lemon-scented Fern**
Oreopteris limbosperma (All.) Holub, synonyms
Thelypteris limbosperma (All.) H. P. Fuchs,
T. oreopteris (Ehrh.) Slosson. Native, common
by streams, roadsides and in woods, on acid
soils in mountain districts. One of the first
things to be noticed is the bright yellowish-
green colour of this fern, especially early in the
season. Otherwise it might be mistaken for a
Male Fern. Another feature is a strong almost
citron scent which is released by brushing past
or rubbing the leaves. Fronds (left) are 30 to
90cm long with two rows of small sori (above)
along the edges on lower sides. Spores ripe
July to August.

Mountain Fern or **Lemon-scented Fern** *Oreopteris limbosperma*

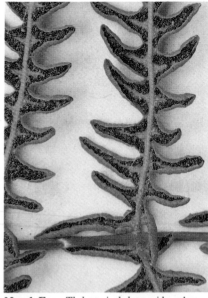

Marsh Fern *Thelypteris thelypteroides* subsp. *glabra*

Photographed 26 July

Marsh Fern *Thelypteris thelypteroides* Michx.
subsp. *glabra* Holub, synonyms *T. palustris*
Schott, *Dryopteris thelypteris* (L.) A. Gray.
A rare native of fens and marshes, scattered
throughout England and Wales, in a few places
in Scotland and in the south-west of Ireland.
The slender, creeping black rhizomes form a
thick underground mat sending up single
fronds of two types: sterile fronds (see left)
which are 15 to 60cm and appear in May or
June and fertile fronds which are 30 to 100cm
and appear about a month later. The fertile
fronds are thicker and produce spores in small
round sori (top) which may be almost hidden
by the inrolled leaf margin. Spores ripe July to
August.

Marsh Fern *Thelypteris thelypteroides* subsp. *glabra*

Holly Fern *Polystichum lonchitis*

Holly Fern *Polystichum lonchitis* (L.) Roth. Native, found in rock clefts on mountains, rarely lower than 300m and indicating base-rich soils. Most frequent in the highlands of Scotland but also recorded from north Wales, west Ireland and north England. The fronds (above) are 15 to 60cm long. Although of thick texture and bearing long almost bristle-like teeth, its name may be misleading as it bears only a passing resemblance to Holly. Young leaves are a brighter green than those from the previous year (see photograph left) and round sori (top) form a neat row around the leaf divisions. Spores ripe June to August.

Holly Fern *Polystichum lonchitis* Photographed 22 June

Hard Shield Fern *Polystichum aculeatum*

Hard Shield Fern *Polystichum aculeatum* Photographed 19 July

Hard Shield Fern *Polystichum aculeatum* (L.) Roth. Native, found throughout Britain in woods, shady places, hedgerows and on shady rock ledges in mountains where it usually indicates a lime-rich soil. Most common in the south-west of Scotland and western England, rare in the north of Scotland and in Ireland. Fronds (above) are 30 to 90cm long, dark glossy green with a hard, almost leathery texture. Sori are shown in top photograph. Spores ripe July to August.

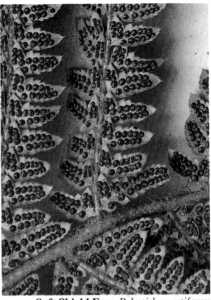

Soft Shield Fern *Polystichum setiferum*

Photographed 26 July

Soft Shield Fern *Polystichum setiferum*
(Forsk.) Woynar. Native, found in woods and
hedgerows, more frequent in the south of
England and in Ireland, scattered elsewhere
and rare in Scotland. Fronds are much softer
than on Hard Shield Fern and are a lighter
colour. They are 30 to 120cm long. The
pinnules (or leaflets) are shortly stalked whereas
on Hard Shield Fern they are stalkless and
often overlap the main stem. Spores ripe July
to August.

Soft Shield Fern *Polystichum setiferum*

Brittle Bladder Fern *Cystopteris fragilis*

Brittle Bladder Fern *Cystopteris fragilis* (L.)
Bernh. Native, growing in rock crevices and
walls. Fairly common in Scotland, north
England, Wales and north and west Ireland,
rare elsewhere. The fronds (above) are 6 to
35cm long with a dark brittle stalk about half
that length. Sori (top) are in two rows on the
underside of each pinnule and are covered
initially by a membranous flap which is swollen
into a bladder shape at the base, hence the
generic name derived from the Greek *kystis*
meaning bladder (this flap is not shown in
photograph). Spores ripe July to August.

Brittle Bladder Fern *Cystopteris fragilis* Photographed 3 July

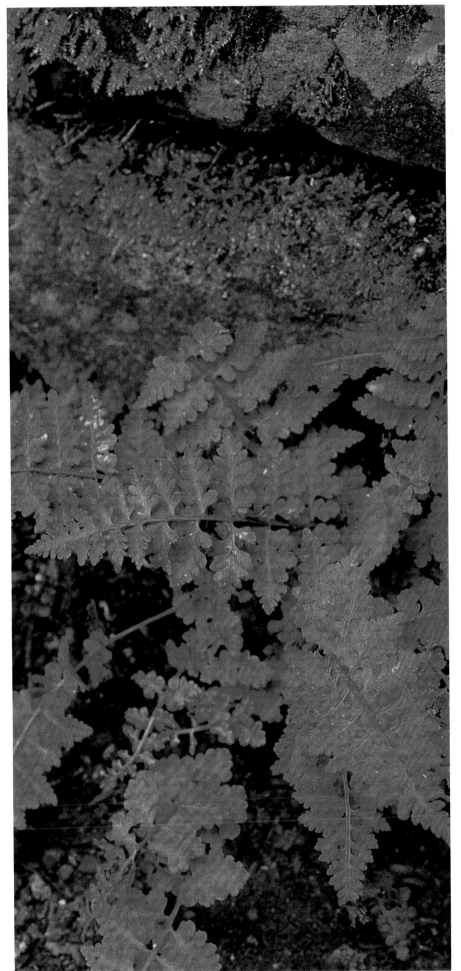

Dickie's Bladder Fern *Cystopteris dickieana*
Sim. Native and rare, found in sea caves on the
north-east coasts of Scotland. Similar to Brittle
Bladder Fern but smaller, with divisions of the
frond overlapping, giving a less 'lacy'
appearance. Spores ripe July to August.

Photographed July

Mountain Bladder Fern *Cystopteris montana*
(Lam.) Desv. Native and rare, growing only on
wet basic rocks in the central highlands of
Scotland though previously found in north
Wales and the Lake District. It has long
creeping rhizomes. The fronds are 10 to 30cm
long with the lowest pair of divisions longer
than the others giving a triangular outline.
Spores ripe July to August.

Dickie's Bladder Fern *Cystopteris dickieana* Photographed 24 July

Bracken or **Brake** *Pteridium aquilinum* Photographed 11 October

Bracken or **Brake** *Pteridium aquilinum*

Photographed 16 June

Bracken or **Brake** *Pteridium aquilinum* (L.)
Kuhn. Native, common throughout Britain in
woods, heaths and grassland on sheltered parts
of hills, usually on acid soil and absent from
limestone. Possibly one of the best known
ferns, also one with the most nuisance value as
a weed. It can be poisonous to livestock if
eaten in quantity but is normally avoided by
cattle, sheep or rabbits and so it spreads in
their grazing areas, reducing their value. The
far-reaching rhizomes make eradication
difficult but selective herbicides have been
developed to aid farmers in its control.
Fronds (left) grow from the root stock singly
and may be anything up to about 180cm in
height and sometimes even more depending on
its conditions. They are triangular in shape
with strong stems almost half the length of the
whole. The sori (top) are distinctive, forming a
thin line around the margin beneath each leaf
segment. When young they are covered by the
inrolled edge and a narrow membrane. Spores
ripe July to August.

Bracken or **Brake** *Pteridium aquilinum*

Oak Fern *Gymnocarpium dryopteris* (L.) Newm., synonym *Thelypteris dryopteris* (L.) Slosson. Native, of shady scree and stream banks and rocky woods. Common in Scotland and north England and north Wales; rare elsewhere. The fronds are 10 to 40cm long, arising singly from black wiry rhizomes, triangular in outline and very thin and delicate in texture. It could only be confused with the limestone fern, which generally has a narrower triangular shape and has a glandular surface. Spores ripe July to August.

Oak Fern *Gymnocarpium dryopteris* Photographed 19 July

Photographed 20 June

Limestone Fern or **Limestone Polypody** *Gymnocarpium robertianum* (Hoffm.) Newn., synonym *Thelypteris robertiana* (Hoffm.) Slosson. Native and rare, found in rocky woods and on scree in the limestone districts of England and Wales with one recorded in Ireland and one in the north of Scotland. Fronds are 15 to 55cm long arising singly from the rhizomes. They are triangular as in Oak Fern but are darker green and glandular giving an almost mealy appearance. Spores ripe July to August.

Beech Fern *Phegopteris connectilis* Photographed 19 July

Beech Fern *Phegopteris connectilis* (Michx.) Watt, synonym *Thelypteris phegopteris* (L.) Slosson. Native, found in damp shady places in woods, by streams and waterfalls. Most frequent in Scotland, north England and north Wales, rare elsewhere. Fronds are 20 to 40cm long with a brittle stalk at least half the length of the whole. Beech Fern has a similar texture to the Oak Fern but is clearly distinguished by shape and the fine white hairs all over the fronds. Both grow in similar situations but the Beech Fern prefers a damper habitat. Spores ripe June to August.

Black Spleenwort *Asplenium adiantum- nigrum*

Photographed 18 July

Black Spleenwort *Asplenium adiantum-nigrum* L. Native, common in rock crevices, walls and rocky banks in all western parts of Britain. Fronds (left) are 10 to 45cm long, narrowly triangular in shape. Stalks are dark and brittle and may run back a long distance in a rock crevice. The leaves are hard, almost leathery, and sori are long and narrow, grouped nearer the centre of leaf divisions. Spores ripe June to October.

Photographed 18 July

Sea Spleenwort *Asplenium marinum* L. Native, found in rock crevices by the sea in north and west Britain and in Ireland. Fronds are 8 to 50cm long and form thick tufts. The photograph shows a young specimen; an older one would have longer fronds with more leaflets. Spores are produced in long, narrow sori similar to other Spleenworts and are ripe between June and October.

Maidenhair Spleenwort *Asplenium trichomanes* L. Native, common in western parts of Britain on rocks and walls usually on basic rock, scattered in the east. Its English name indicates a similarity to the Maidenhair Fern but the two ferns could not be confused when seen together. Fronds (above) are 5 to 35cm with shiny black stalks and hard dark green leaflets. Sori are long and narrow. Spores ripe May to October.

Photographed 16 October

Forked Spleenwort *Asplenium septentrionale* (L.) Hoffm. Native, rare, found in rock crevices, never limestone, in the mountains of north Wales, north England and sometimes in lowland Scotland. The narrow forked fronds are 5 to 15cm long with dark shiny stalks. The sori are long and narrow, from one to five on each segment, appearing to merge into one another. Spores ripe June to October.

Maidenhair Spleenwort *Asplenium trichomanes* Photographed 3 July

Green Spleenwort *Asplenium viride* Photographed 14 August

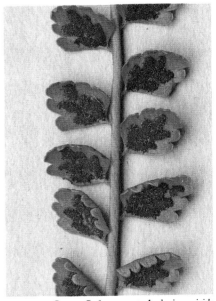

Green Spleenwort *Asplenium viride*

Green Spleenwort *Asplenium viride* Huds.
Native, common on limestone rocks in
mountain or hill districts of Wales, north
England and Scotland and a few localities in
the west of Ireland. Similar to Maidenhair
Spleenwort but has a green stem and is more
delicate in appearance. Sori (top) are long and
narrow as in other spleenworts. Spores ripe
June to September.

Hart's Tongue *Asplenium scolopendrium* L., synonym *Phyllitis scolopendrium* (L.) Newm. Native, common except in mountains of Scotland. It grows in woods and hedgerows, on shady walls or rocks, preferring a calcareous substrate. Fronds are 10 to 60cm long, undivided, tapering to a point with a heart-shaped base. Sori are long and narrow in opposite pairs. Spores ripe July to August.

Rusty-back Fern Photographed 20 July

Rusty-back Fern *Asplenium ceterach* L., synonym *Ceterach officinarum* DC. Native, growing in cracks in limestone and in mortared walls, most common in the south and west. The underside of the fronds are covered with silvery scales which become rust-coloured with age. Sori are produced among these. Once used as a herbal remedy against spleen and liver disorders. Spores ripe April to October.

Hart's Tongue *Asplenium scolopendrium* Photographed 30 May

Photographed 4 September
Wall Rue *Asplenium ruta-muraria*

Wall Rue *Asplenium ruta-muraria* L. Native, common on walls, bridges and rocks, especially limestone. Often forming thick masses in suitable habitats. Common throughout Britain but less frequent in the east of England and north of Scotland. It was once used as a herbal remedy for rickets. Fronds (above) are 2 to 15cm long and irregular in shape. They may have narrower divisions than those shown. Sori are long and thin, and appear to merge into each other when the spores ripen. Spores ripe June to October.

Wall Rue *Asplenium ruta-muraria* Photographed 9 June

Parsley Fern *Cryptogramma crispa* (L.) Hook. Native, found on scree, walls and bridges, most common in the Lake District, north Wales, and hilly parts of Scotland. Two different types of frond are produced (above); the fertile ones are narrower and longer, 11 to 30cm, sterile ones shorter and more parsley-like are 7 to 15cm. Spores are protected by rolled-under edges of the fronds and are ripe June to August.

Photographed 26 March

Annual Gymnogram or **Jersey Fern** *Anogramma leptaphylla* (L.) Link. Native but rare, found in Jersey and Guernsey. Unusual among ferns in that it is annual. Sterile and fertile fronds are less distinct from each other than in Parsley Fern and are about 10cm long. Sori are in clusters on the underside of fronds and the edges are not rolled under to cover them. Spores ripe March to May.

Parsley Fern *Cryptogramma crispa* Photographed 19 July

Hard Fern *Blechnum spicant* (L.) Roth.
Native, found throughout Britain in shady
woods, hedgerows and rock ledges on acid
soils. Infrequent in central and eastern
England. Sterile fronds are 10 to 40cm long
and lie flat on the ground making a rosette.
Fertile stems are 15 to 75cm and stand erect.
They are narrower and look like a fish
backbone. The fertile fronds die back in winter,
but the sterile ones remain evergreen. Spores
ripe June to August.

Hard Fern *Blechnum spicant* Photographed 16 August

Royal Fern *Osmunda regalis* Photographed 29 June

Royal Fern *Osmunda regalis* L. Native, found in wet bogs in western parts of Britain and elsewhere in fens. A clearly distinctive fern which is often cultivated in gardens for its beautiful stately appearance. Fronds are 60 to 160cm tall in a dense bushy clump. Most are sterile but a few in the centre of the group are usually fertile and these project above the rest. They have upper leaflets narrowed and covered with brown spore-producing structures. Spores ripe June to August.

Common Polypody *Polypodium vulgare* L. Native, common throughout Britain on wall tops, trees and rocks, though less frequent in central and eastern England and Ireland. The fronds (above) are 10 to 40cm long, flat and oblong, with lobes more or less equal in size, and are produced in early summer among older darker fronds from the previous year. The sori are circular and spores ripen in July to August.
Southern Polypody *P. australe* Fée grows on limestone or mortared walls in warmer western parts of Britain. Its fronds are 20 to 50cm long and are much broader than Common Polypody. The lobes are slightly toothed, new fronds appear in late summer or autumn. Sori are oval in outline. Spores ripe August to December.
Intermediate Polypody *P. interjectum* Shivas is found throughout Britain in damp limestone on walls often near the sea. It has characters intermediate between the other two Polypodies with fronds lance-shaped but not as wide as Southern Polypody. New fronds appear in the summer. Sori are oval. Spores ripe July to December.

Common Polypody *Polypodium vulgare* Photographed 18 July

105

Alpine Woodsia *Woodsia alpina* (Bolton)
S.F. Gray. Native, but very rare, on damp
rocks in high mountains in Scotland and north
Wales. Fronds are 3 to 15cm long, narrow with
triangular leaflets, which are less scaly and less
deeply lobed than Oblong Woodsia. Sori are
rounded with a fringe of tiny scales, formed at
leaf margins. Spores ripe July to August.

Photographed July

Oblong Woodsia *Woodsia ilvensis* (L.) R. Br.
Native and rare, on damp rocks in mountains
of Scotland, north England and north Wales.
Fronds 5 to 15cm long, with scales and hairs on
stalks. Broader than Alpine Woodsia with
similar sori. Spores ripe July to August.

Maidenhair Fern *Adiantum capillus-veneris*
L. Native but rare, found on limestone sea
cliffs in a few western localities. Commonly
grown as a house plant but a rare sight in the
wild. Shiny, wiry stems with delicate leaflets.
Up to 30cm long. Spores are produced on the
underside of tiny leaf lobes which curl over to
cover them. Spores ripe May to September.

Maidenhair Fern *Adiantum capillus-veneris* Photographed 19 July

Photographed January

Killarney Fern or **Bristle Fern** *Trichomanes speciosum* Willd. Native and rare, growing on rocks by streams in Killarney, and a few other places. Fronds are 7 to 35cm long with long winged stems. Spores produced around a bristle inside a cup-shaped structure. Spores ripe July to September.

Photographed August

Moonwort *Botrychium lunaria* (L.) Swartz. Native on dry grassland and mountain rock ledges. Lobed sterile fronds are 5 to 20cm with branched spore structures arising near the base. Alchemists believed it could turn mercury to silver. Spores ripe June to August.

Adder's Tongue *Ophioglossum vulgatum* L. Native, found on damp grassland throughout Britain, though least common in Scotland. A supposed similarity to a snake's tongue led to a belief that it could be used as an antidote for snake bites. Height from 5 to 20cm, the top 4 to 6cm of stem bearing the spore cases. Spores ripe May to August.

Adder's Tongue *Ophioglossum vulgatum* Photographed July

Wilson's Filmy Fern *Hymenophyllum wilsonii*

Photographed 19 July

Wilson's Filmy Fern *Hymenophyllum wilsonii* Hook. Native, found in western parts of Britain, more common in Scotland and the Lake District. It grows in wet shady habitats: rocks or trees by rivers or under dripping water. Fronds are up to about 10cm long divided into narrow segments which curl back. Sori are enclosed by two untoothed scales. Spores ripe June to July.

Photographed May

Tunbridge Filmy Fern *Hymenophyllum tunbrigense* (L.) Sm. Native, similar to Wilson's Filmy Fern, and growing in similar shady habitats, rare. Fronds are up to about 10cm long, lighter green than Wilson's Filmy Fern and with flat leaflets. Sori are encased by scales with toothed edges (but not shown in photograph). Spores ripe June to July.

Water Fern *Azolla filiculoides* Lam.
Introduced from warm regions of North
America now naturalized in ponds and ditches
in England, Wales and east Ireland. The
floating fronds are 1 to 2cm across and form
dense masses often turning red in winter. Hair-
like roots hang down into the water. Sori are
tiny and produced in pairs at the base of side
branches. Spores ripe June to September.

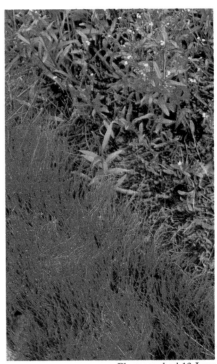

Photographed 13 June
Pillwort *Pilularia globulifera*

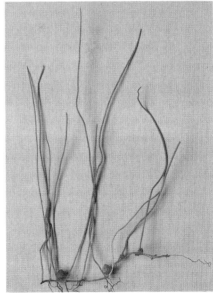

Pillwort *Pilularia globulifera* L. Native,
scattered throughout Britain, but often glossed
over as a grass or young rush (top). It grows in
mud by lakes, ponds, slow rivers and in ditches.
Leaves are 3 to 10cm long and cylindrical,
unfolding from a coiled tip like other ferns.
Spores are produced in spherical hairy capsules,
or 'pills' at the leaf bases; spores ripe June to
September.

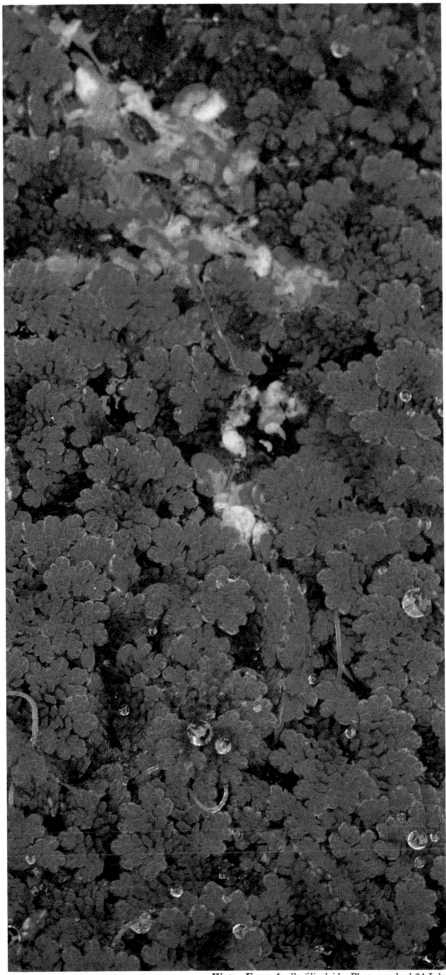

Water Fern *Azolla filiculoides* Photographed 24 July

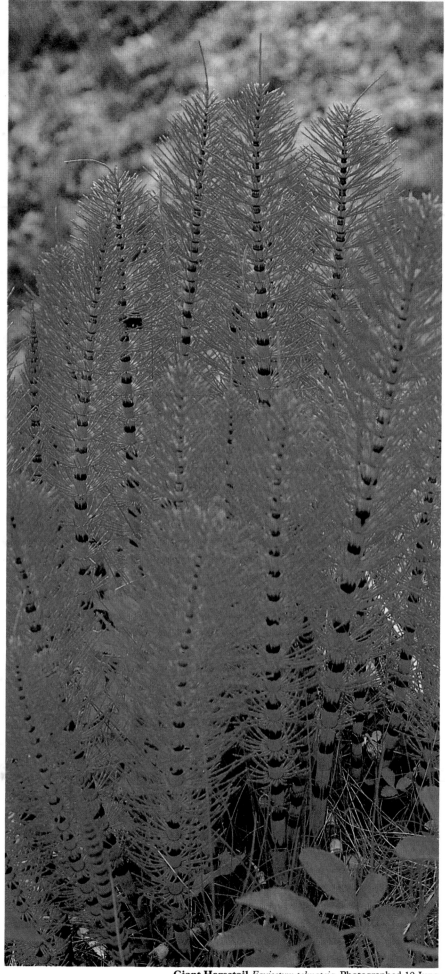

Giant Horsetail *Equisetum telmateia* Photographed 10 June

Giant Horsetail *Equisetum telmateia* Ehrh.
Native perennial with downy rhizomes. Rare in
Scotland, widespread elsewhere, generally on
shady banks on base-rich, heavy, often marshy
soils. Fertile stems are pinkish-brown (above),
about 20 to 40cm tall, larger than Common
Horsetail. Sterile stems (right: showing young
stems) are 100 to 200cm, whitish with twenty
to forty fine grooves. Spores ripe April.

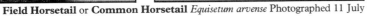

Field Horsetail or **Common Horsetail** *Equisetum arvense* Photographed 11 July

Photographed 5 June

L. Native perennial with hairy rhizomes. Common throughout Britain in fields, wasteground, roadsides and gardens where it may become a troublesome weed. Two different types of stem are produced (above left): pinkish-brown fertile stems appear in March and are 10 to 25cm tall. These stems die back when spores produced in the 'cone' have ripened. Sterile green stems appear as the 'cone' is ripening and may be 20 to 80cm tall, with between six and twelve grooves and as many spreading branches from most of the upper joints. A cross-section of the green stems reveals a central hollow less than half the diameter of the whole. All horsetails are poisonous to livestock. Spores ripe March to June.

Equisetum x litorale Kuhlew. ex Rupr. A hybrid between Field Horsetail and Water Horsetail, found throughout Britain, but often mistaken for one of the parent species. It is intermediate in character, with a stem hollow larger than Field Horsetail, and smaller than Water Horsetail. Stem grooves are shallower than Field Horsetail and the sheaths are looser than Water Horsetail.

Water Horsetail *Equisetum fluviatile* Photographed 9 June

Water Horsetail *Equisetum fluviatile* L.

Native perennial with glossy purplish rhizomes, common throughout Britain in marshes, swamps and lake and riversides, often in huge masses covering large areas of pond or lake (left). Fertile and sterile stems are similar except for the 'cone' produced at the tip of fertile ones. Stems are smooth and may be sparsely covered with branches or completely bare (see both photographs). The central

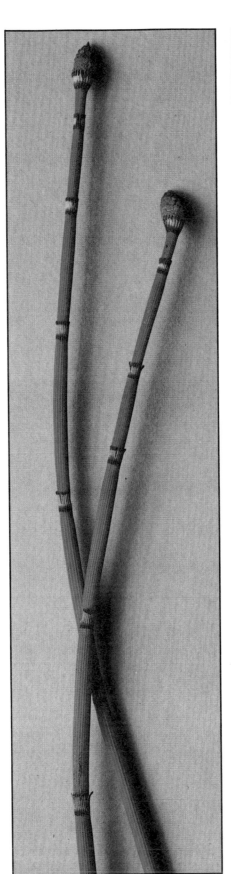

Water Horsetail *Equisetum fluviatile*

Photographed 7 June

Photographed 9 June

hollow is larger than in any other horsetail and fills up to four-fifths of the stem. Height from 50 to 140cm. Spores ripe June to July.

Dutch Rush *Equisetum hyemale* L. Native perennial, scattered throughout Britain. Found in wet shady places. The stems are hard and rough and each joint has a broad white band, two narrower black bands and between ten and thirty blunt teeth. Once imported from the Netherlands to use as pot scourers. Height from 30 to 100cm. Spores are produced in 'cones' at stem tips from June to August.

Marsh Horsetail *Equisetum palustre* L. Native perennial with smooth rhizomes and oval tubers; common throughout Britain in bogs, wet heaths, woods and meadows. The central hollow is smaller than Field Horsetail and both fertile and sterile stems are green. They have four to eight deep grooves. Height from 10 to 60cm. Spores are produced in 'cones' at tips of fertile stems from May to July.

113

Wood Horsetail *Equisetum sylvaticum* Photographed 22 August

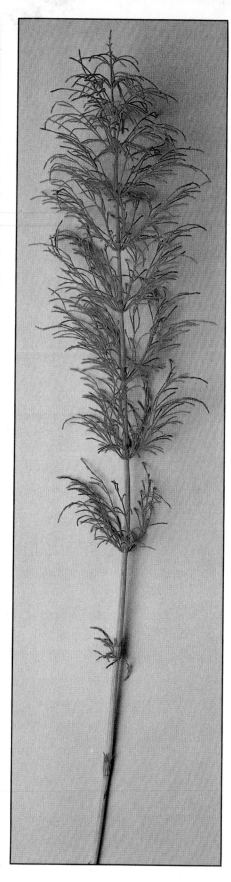

Wood Horsetail *Equisetum sylvaticum* L.
Native perennial, common in damp woods,
moors and swamps on acid soils in Scotland,
north England and north Ireland. The stem
branches are themselves branched and droop,
giving a distinctive feathery appearance. Height
from 10 to 80cm. Fertile stems (not shown)
are similar, but smaller with an oval 'cone' at
the tip, ripe April to May.

Photographed March
Land Quillwort *Isoetes histrix*

Photographed 15 August

Photographed 13 July

Land Quillwort *Isoetes histrix* Bory. Native, rare, found in the Lizard district of Cornwall and the Channel Isles, almost buried in peaty or sandy soil which dries out in summer. The leaves grow in thick tufts with swollen bases and are 1 to 3cm long. Spores are produced in tiny structures at the leaf bases and are ripe April to May (see both photographs above).

Quillwort *Isoetes lacustris* L. Native aquatic plant, growing submerged at the edge of stony lakes and tarns. Most common in the mountain regions of Wales and north England and scattered through Scotland and Ireland. Soft, dark leaves 10 to 30cm tall. Cross-section shows four channels. Spores ripe May to July.

Lesser Clubmoss *Selaginella selaginoides* (L.) Link. Native, quite common on wet rocks and by streams in mountain areas of north-west Britain. The creeping stems send up erect branches with tiny pointed leaves. Spores are produced at the bases of slightly toothed, larger leaves at the stem tips. Spores ripe June to August.

Fir Clubmoss *Huperzia selago* (L.) Bernh., synonym *Lycopodium selago* L. Native, common on mountain moorland, heath, grassland and rock ledges. Spores are not produced in a 'cone' but in small structures in the leaf axils. The upright growth habit helps to distinguish it from Stag's-horn Moss. Spores ripe June to August.

115

Alpine Clubmoss *Diphasiastrum alpinum* (L.) Holub *Lycopodium alpinum* L. Native, found on moors and grassland in the mountains of Scotland, north England, Wales and Ireland. The stems are four-sided and branched (left), and some produce small yellow 'cones' (see above) which contain the spores. Spores ripe June to August.

Alpine Clubmoss *Diphasiastrum alpinum* Photographed 22 June

Stag's-horn Clubmoss *Lycopodium clavatum*
L. Native, common on mountain moors,
heaths and grassland in Scotland and Wales.
Stems are densely packed with hair-tipped
narrow leaves (left) and creep along the ground
rooting at intervals. Fruiting 'cones' (above)
usually grow in pairs, and produce bright
yellow spores known as lycopodium powder.
Spores ripe June to September.

Stag's-horn Clubmoss *Lycopodium clavatum* Photographed 15 August

Polytrichum commune

Polytrichum commune

Polytrichum formosum Hedw. Commonly forming extensive patches on sandy acidic heaths, moors and woodland. Smaller than *P. commune* with four or five-sided fruit capsules frequently found in the summer. Height to about 10cm.

Polytrichum piliferum

Polytrichum commune Hedw. Common, forms dark green deep tufts (left) in wet heaths, bogs, moorland and by streams in woodland. Height from 2 to 40cm; distinguished by dark green toothed leaves on long stems in the above habitats. Capsules (above and top) are frequently found in the summer and are four-sided, with yellowish hairy caps when young. Male plants have a pinkish rosette of leaves at their tips (top).

Polytrichum piliferum

Polytrichum piliferum Hedw. Common on well drained acidic or neutral soil on rocks, moors and heaths. It grows in greyish-green patches, each plant to about 6cm tall. The leaves have silvery hair points and are crowded together towards the top of the stem in a brush-like manner. Male plants (left) bear bright reddish rosette-like structures; females produce slightly inclined capsules (top) on red stalks.

Polytrichum juniperinum Hedw. Common on dry acidic soil on heaths and moors and on rocks and walls. It forms greyish patches of plants 1 to 7cm tall with orange-red leaf-tips. Fruiting is frequent, four-sided capsules with red lids produced on red stalks in summer. Male plants are shown in the photograph and are conspicuous with their rosette of orange or red tinted leaves.

Pogonatum nanum (Hedw.) P. Beauv., synonym *Polytrichum nanum* Hedw. Throughout Britain on acid soil on banks. About 2cm in height with toothed leaves and short, urn-shaped capsules on stalks 1.5 to 3cm. *P. aloides*, a much commoner plant in similar situations, has longer, cylindrical capsules. Fruits are common in autumn and winter, pale with white caps.

Andreaea rothii Web. & Mohr. Common on rocks, scree and walls in mountain districts, found at lower altitudes in the north and west of Scotland. Plants are 0.5 to 1.5cm. The dark tufts look similar to *A. rupestris* but the leaves are narrower and long, pointed and often more strongly curved. Fruiting is not common but with characteristic four-valved capsules produced in spring and summer.

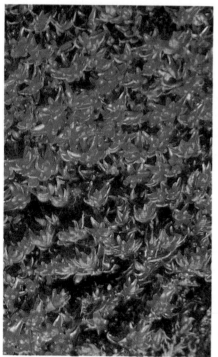

Andreaea rupestris Hedw. Common in the mountain districts of Britain on rocks, scree, cliffs and walls. Forms small, low, brown tufts, height from 0.5 to 3cm. The small, rather blunt leaves are usually attached at about 45° to stem. Spores are often produced and are ripe in the summer.

Tetraphis pellucida Hedw. Common on rotting stumps and logs and sometimes on peat banks. It forms patches of upright stems with broad, oval leaves. Height from 0.5 to 1.5cm. Fruiting capsules are not common but are produced on stalks about 1cm tall; they are erect with four teeth. More common are vegetative reproductive structures in small cups at the tips of stalks, a distinctive feature of this moss.

Seligeria paucifolia (Dicks.) Carruthers. Common in parts of south England on chalk fragments under trees and other shaded sites. Plants are very small, forming thin bright green patches probably most noticeable in early summer when they are covered with capsules on short yellow stalks. The photograph is a very close up view.

Atrichum undulatum   *Ceratodon purpureus*   *Dicranella heteromalla*

Atrichum undulatum (Hedw.) P. Beauv. Sometimes named Catherine's Moss because of an association with Catherine the Great of Russia. It is common on damp soil in woods, heaths and on stream banks. Plants can reach 7cm in length and have delicate wavy leaves strongly crimped when dry. Long curved fruit capsules are produced on red stalks in spring. Long beaked lids fall when ripe.

Ceratodon purpureus (Hedw.) Brid. Common throughout Britain on lime-free soil in fields, woodland and in towns. Plants are up to about 3cm tall and may be green or reddish-brown. Fruit capsules are reddish-brown on purple stalks and are produced, often in great abundance, in the spring.

Dicranella heteromalla (Hedw.) Schimp. Common and forms patches on banks, ditches, woodland and tree stumps on acidic soils. Plants are deep green, 1 to 3cm tall. Extremely long and narrow leaves are strongly curved all in the same direction. Fruit capsules (above) are common, produced in winter and spring on yellow stalks.

Dicranoweisia cirrata

Dicranum scoparium

Dicranoweisia cirrata (Hedw.) Lindb. Common in lowland Britain on trees, logs, walls and thatching; rare in the north of Scotland and Ireland. Plants are 0.5 to 2cm tall, with long narrow leaves which become curved when dry. Fruiting may be common, with pale erect narrow capsules produced on yellow stalks in autumn through to spring.

Dicranum scoparium Hedw. (top right) Common on many substrates such as soil, rocks, trees and rotting stumps on acid soils. Plants reach about 10cm and the many leaves tend to be curved in one direction. Fruit capsules are more common in wetter regions of Britain. Their stalks are yellowish with a reddish base, and always borne singly (above).

Dicranum majus Sm. Common on acidic ground on soil, rocks or rotting wood in the north and west; rare in south-east and central England. Plants may reach 15cm in height and leaves are densely set and curved in one direction. Fruit capsules are sometimes produced in the wetter regions of Britain and are borne on yellowish stalks, often several together.

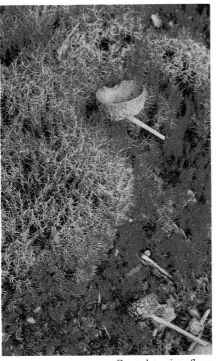

Campylopus introflexus   *Leucobryum glaucum*   *Fissidens adianthoides*

Campylopus introflexus (Hedw.) Brid.
Introduced into Europe from the Southern
Hemisphere, first found in Sussex in 1941.
Now frequent throughout Britain except central
and east England. Usually on peat, clay, rotting
wood or tree stumps. Height 0.5 to 5cm. The
most striking feature of this moss is that when
dry a star is formed at the shoot tips by long
silvery hairs. Fruits small, several on one plant,
produced in spring.

Leucobryum glaucum (Hedw.) Angstr. Whitish
or bluish-green cushions, common on rocks,
tree stumps, and on the ground in woodland,
heaths and bogs, usually on acid soils.
Particularly characteristic of beech woods.
Height to 15cm. The blue colour and close
dense cushions make this species easily
distinguishable. Fruit capsules are rarely
produced, but appear in autumn.

Fissidens adianthoides Hedw. Common on wet
rock ledges near streams, in fens and non-acid
grassland. Plants are about 5cm long, more or
less erect, with many tongue-shaped leaves
closely set in two rows to make flat fronds.
Fruit capsules are produced in autumn to
spring. They are erect or curved with a
reddish stalk.

Fissidens taxifolius

Encalypta streptocarpa Hedw. Common on mortar in old walls and on calcareous rocks or soil, forming bright yellowish-green tufts or patches. Plants are about 2cm tall with flat tongue-shaped leaves forming a rosette shape at the tip and curling when dry Fruit capsules are very rare, produced in spring and are spirally ribbed. *E. vulgaris* is occasional on basic rocks and walls. It is smaller and has capsules covered by tiny white caps.

Tortula ruralis (Hedw.) Gaertn., Meyer & Scherb. subsp. *ruraliformis* (Besch.) Dix. Common on sand dunes and sometimes found inland on sandy soil. It forms large orange-brown patches of plants 1 to 4cm tall. Leaves curve outwards, and are pointed with hair tips. Fruit capsules are curved and when ripe discard the lid to reveal a fringe of teeth. They are produced in spring or early summer on reddish stalks.

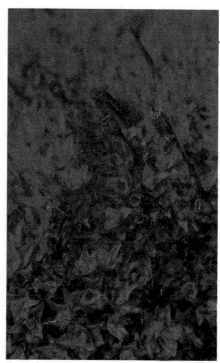

Fissidens taxifolius Hedw. Common on soils in woodland, fields, roadsides and disturbed ground. Plants are 1 to 2cm tall with crenulate leaves. Fruit capsules are horizontal on red stalks arising from the bases of the shoots, produced in winter. *Fissidens bryoides*, a common plant in similar habitats to *F. taxifolius* is smaller, has narrow, pale borders edging the leaves. The fruit capsules grow from the ends of the shoots.

Tortula muralis Hedw. Common on walls and other man-made habitats in country and towns, sometimes on limestone or sandstone. It forms small cushions usually less than 1cm tall. Leaves are oblong and have long hairs at their tips, straight when moist and spirally curled when dry. Fruit capsules are common in spring and summer. When ripe a protective hood and lid fall off to reveal spirally twisted hairs.

Pottia heimii (Hedw.) Furnr. Fairly common in salt marshes and on rocks and soil near the sea, rarely found inland. Plants are larger than *P. truncata* and have fruit capsules on reddish-brown stalks up to 0.9cm tall. They are produced in spring and early summer and turn rusty red when ripe.

Tortella tortuosa

Barbula convoluta

Pottia truncata (Hedw.) Furnr. Most common in the south, found on heavy acid soil in fields, waste places and gardens. Plants are only 0.3 to 0.5cm tall and are usually fertile. Fruit capsules are erect, borne on yellowish stalks about 0.3 to 0.6cm long and are produced mainly in winter and early spring. Capsules are short, wine-glass shaped and have no teeth.

Tortella tortuosa (Hedw.) Limpr. Common on limestone rocks and grassland, in hills and mountains of Britain. Plants are 1 to 8cm tall, yellowish, with long narrow leaves which have wavy edges. Leaves are strongly curled when dry; with glossy midribs. Fruit capsules are rare, produced in the summer on yellowish-red stalks.

Barbula convoluta Hedw. Common on wall tops, pavement cracks, waste-ground and fields, forming mats or cushions. Plants are matt pale green or yellowish, 0.2 to 0.5cm tall with flat leaves, strongly curled when dry. Fruit capsules are cylindrical and erect on yellow stalks. When the lid falls, spirally twisted teeth are exposed. They are uncommon and produced in the spring and summer.

Grimmia pulvinata

Barbula cylindrica (Tayl.) Schimp. Forms patches or scattered stems on waste-ground, paths, walls and fields. Plants are about 1.5cm tall, usually yellow-brown, and are similar to *B. convoluta* but with triangular leaves. Fruit capsules have wavy reddish stalks and are occasionally produced in winter and spring.

Trichostomum brachydontium Bruch. Common on rocks and wall-tops, especially on the west coast, near the sea. Plants are 1 to 4cm tall with long, tongue-shaped leaves which become twisted when dry. Fruit capsules are very rare; they are fragile and produced on yellow stalks.

Cinclidotus fontinaloides (Hedw.) P. Beauv. Frequent on rock or wood submerged or near lakes, streams and rivers. Branched stems may be 12cm long, forming dull, dark green tufts. Leaves are long and narrow, with thickened edges, spread outwards near the shoot tips. Fruit capsules are occasionally produced in spring hidden among the leaves. They are erect and have reddish rims; the conical lids fall to reveal spirally twisted hairs.

Schistidium apocarpum (Hedw.) Br. Eur., synonym *Grimmia apocarpa* Hedw. Common on calcareous rocks, walls and concrete, rarely found in non-basic areas. Plants are about 0.5 to 6cm tall, may be green or more commonly brownish, and have hair-like tips. Fruit capsules have little or no stalks, bright red teeth, and are commonly produced in winter and spring.

Grimmia pulvinata (Hedw.) Sm. Common in lowland Britain forming thick round cushions on walls, roofs, rocks and mortar. Plants are up to about 3cm and leaves have long silvery hair tips which give the whole clump a greyish hairy appearance. Fruit capsules are common and are borne on strongly curved stalks which gradually straighten with age. They are produced in the spring.

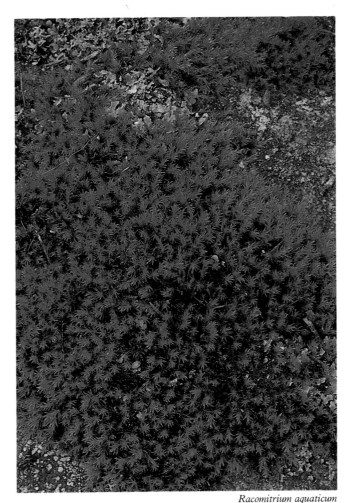

Dryptodon patens

Racomitrium aquaticum

Schistidium maritimum (Turn.) Br. Eur., synonym *Grimmia maritima* Turn. Found on acidic rocks on west and north coasts of Britain, forming dark green tufts or cushions just above high tide mark. Plants are up to about 2cm tall and leaves are dark green and become strongly curled when dry. Fruit capsules are common and produced on very short stalks, about 1cm long, in winter.

Dryoptodon patens (Hedw.) Brid., synonym *Grimmia patens* (Hedw.) Br. Eur. Uncommon, found in mountain districts on damp rocks at high altitudes. Plants are 2 to 10cm tall and form loose dull green or yellowish patches of upright or drooping stems. It may be taken for *Racomitrium aquaticum* but its leaves have two distinctive wings on the undersides of their midribs. Fruit capsules are rare, produced in spring on arched yellow stalks.

Racomitrium aquaticum (Schrad.) Brid. Uncommon generally, but frequent on acidic rocks by mountain streams. Plants are 2 to 12cm tall and form thick yellowish tufts or patches. Leaves are long, narrowing to blunt tips with no hair points, which gives this moss a quite different appearance to many other rock-dwelling *Racomitrium* species. Cylindrical fruit capsules are occasionally produced in spring.

Racomitrium lanuginosum

Funaria hygrometrica

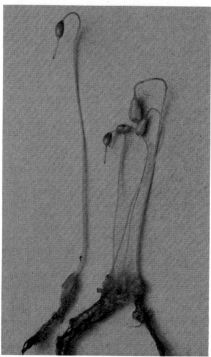

Racomitrium lanuginosum (Hedw.) Brid. Common in hill and mountain districts on acidic rock and peat. It forms a distinctive mountain-top community known as 'racomitrium heath' where it grows in extensive greyish mats. Plants are up to about 15cm with branching stems and hair-pointed leaves often curved in one direction. Fruit capsules are small and cylindrical; occasionally produced in spring on rough stalks.

Ptychomitrium polyphyllum (Sw.) Br. Eur. Common on acidic rocks and wall tops in western and northern Britain, absent from central and southern England. Plants reach about 4cm tall and have wavy leaves which become strongly curled and twisted when dry. Fruit capsules are common and produced in late spring and early summer.

Funaria hygrometrica Hedw. Common on disturbed ground, fields, open woodland and heaths especially on fire sites and a common weed in greenhouses and gardens, forming large masses of green and orange when fruit capsules are ripe. Plants are about 1.5cm tall and fruit capsules are common, produced in autumn and winter. Their stalks are yellow and may become strongly curved with age.

Physcomitrium pyriforme (Hedw.) Brid. Frequently found on damp bare ground in damp fields, waste places, ditches and stream sides. Plants reach about 0.5cm, with oval, pointed leaves, resembling *Funaria hygrometrica* but with erect pear-shaped fruit capsules on short stalks. They are common and produced from late winter to summer.

Splachnum ampullaceum Hedw. Fairly frequent in west and north Britain, rare in central and south-east England. It forms tufts on dung on heaths, moorland and bogs. Plants reach 3cm tall and have toothed, tapering leaves. Fruit capsules are erect, with deep red stalks and are commonly produced during the summer. They are shaped like old wine bottles with swollen bases and cylindrical tops.

Orthodontium lineare

Splachnum sphaericum Hedw. Fairly frequent in the west and north of Britain, especially in hilly districts. It forms tufts on dung, especially sheep droppings, in hill pasture. Looks similar to *S. ampullaceum* but the capsules have more nearly spherical bases. They are mainly found in the summer.

Schistostega pennata (Hedw.) Web. & Mohr. Found in sandstone areas at entrances to caves, mine shafts or burrows, particularly in the West Country. The delicate, flat fronds are about 1.5cm tall, arising from thin, glistening green threads (protonema) which appear to glow in dark habitats. The soft, translucent leaves are in two flat rows. Small round fruit capsules are occasionally produced in spring and summer.

Orthodontium lineare Schwaegr. Introduced moss, native to the Southern Hemisphere, first recorded in Yorkshire in 1922. Now spread almost throughout Britain, on peat banks, tree bases and rotting wood. Height to about 1cm. The long, narrow leaves are slightly curved back but not as regularly as in *Dicranella* species. Fruit capsules are horizontal, narrowly club shaped, common, produced in spring.

Pohlia nutans

Bryum capillare

Pohlia carnea (Schimp.) Lindb., synonym *P. deliculata* (Hedw.) Grout. Frequent in lowland regions on damp clay soils, particularly on stream and river banks. Plants are up to 1cm tall with delicate oval leaves, shorter and more rounded near the stem bases. Fruit capsules are occasional, but may be abundant. They are horizontal or hanging with a ring of orange-red teeth when ripe; produced in winter and spring on short stalks.

Pohlia nutans (Hedw.) Lindb. Common on heath, moor, peat banks and sometimes in woodland and on rotting stumps. Often found on old industrial sites, especially lead mine waste, never on calcareous or limestone soils. Height 1 to 7.5cm. Capsules may be produced in abundance on bright orange or red stalks. They are green at first, becoming pale orange-brown, and point downwards.

Bryum capillare Hedw. Common throughout Britain forming green or red-tinged patches on rocks, walls, trees and sometimes on soil. Plants are 1 to 5cm tall with tiny leaves which become twisted when dry. Fruiting is frequent in spring and summer with slightly drooping tubular to pear-shaped capsules.

Bryum algovicum Sendtn. ex C.Mull. var. *rutheanum* (Warnst.) Crundw., synonym *B. pendulum* (Hornsch.) Schimp. Found on sand dunes, also inland on sandy or gravelly banks, walls and rock crevices. It grows to about 1.5cm tall and can only be definitely identified when its fruit is present. These are common, produced in spring and have drooping pear-shaped capsules.

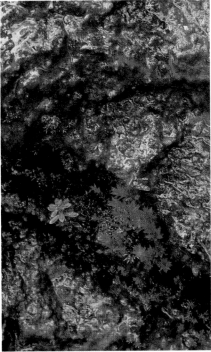

Bryum pseudotriquetrum

Rhizomnium punctatum

Bryum argenteum Hedw. Common on pavements, walls, compacted soil etc, in towns and on rocks and cliff ledges elsewhere. It is easily recognized by its silvery catkin-like stems. Height from 1 to 1.5cm, often smaller. Fruits are produced in autumn through to spring and are not common. They are small and drooping on a short stalk about 1cm tall; reddish-brown or crimson when ripe.

Bryum pseudotriquetrum (Hedw.) Schwaegr. Common in marshes, bogs, fens, dune slacks and mountain wet flushes. It grows in thick dark tufts, often tinged reddish and covered with reddish-brown hairs on the lower stems. Plants may reach about 15cm in height. Fruiting bodies are not common, produced in autumn and spring, 4 to 5mm long, on tall stalks. Male organs form rosette-like clusters on separate stems.

Rhizomnium punctatum (Hedw.) Kop., synonym *Mnium punctatum* Hedw. Common on damp shady ground and rocks by mountain and woodland streams. Plants may reach 10cm. The translucent, pale green or bright red, round leaves have thickened edges and may be covered with tiny dots. Male plants form rosette-like clusters of leaves at their tips and female ones produce fruiting capsules on long reddish stalks in autumn and winter.

Mnium hornum

Plagiomnium affine

Plagiomnium undulatum

Mnium hornum Hedw. One of the commonest woodland mosses, found throughout Britain on tree-bases, rotting wood, peat and rock ledges. Plants are 2 to 10cm tall and have male and female parts on separate plants. These are shown in the photograph: males clustered into a rosette-like structure, females forming hanging fruiting capsules on long red stalks in spring. These are fairly common.

Plagiomnium affine (Funck) Kop., synonym *Mnium affine* Funck. Frequent in most of England on damp soil in woodland; rare elsewhere. Plants may grow to about 10cm, though usually much less. Leaves are broad and toothed. Male plants form rosettes of leaves, similar to *Mnium hornum* and females produce drooping fruit capsules on red stalks. These are very rare and produced in the spring.

Plagiomnium undulatum (Hedw.) Kop., synonym *Mnium undulatum* Hedw. Common in damp shady places by streams, in woods and dune slacks. Stems may grow to as much as 10cm. The upper leaves are long, translucent light green and wavy. Male and female structures are on separate plants, the male plants forming rosette-like structures. Fruit capsules are occasionally produced in spring, usually several on each plant.

Aulacomnium androgynum

Aulacomnium palustre

Plagiomnium rostratum (Schrad.) Kop., synonym *Mnium longirostrum* Brid. Found throughout Britain, forming loose green patches in shady places on soil and wood in woodland and by streams or marshes. The mainly prostrate, straggly-branched stems may grow to about 5cm and have translucent oval or round leaves with toothed edges. Fruit capsules are frequent in spring, two often being produced at the same point.

Aulacomnium androgynum (Hedw.) Schwaegr. Common on damp humus-capped rocks, peat and rotting wood in the south and east of England; rare elsewhere. Plants are about 2.5 to 3.5cm long, with matted hairs at their bases. Leaves are oblong and pointed, smaller than *A. palustre*. Fruit capsules are very rare, produced in spring and summer. Vegetative reproductive structures (gemmae) are common, produced in round, yellowish-green clusters.

Aulacomnium palustre (Hedw.) Schwaegr. Common on moors and forming tufts in bogs, wet flushes and heaths. Plants may reach about 10cm or more in length, the stems matted together with brown felted filaments (rhizoids). Leaves are pale straw-coloured, oblong, bluntly pointed and become twisted when dry. Fruits are occasionally produced in summer on long stalks.

Philonotis fontana

Orthotrichum anomalum

Bartramia pomiformis Hedw. Common in rock crevices, walls and banks in upland districts, occasionally found in south-east and central England. Plants may reach 8cm, are bluish-green and covered with reddish-brown hairs below. Leaves are long and narrow with toothed edges. Fruit capsules are common, produced in summer on shiny, red stalks, and resemble tiny green apples.

Bartramia ithyphylla Brid. Less common than *B. pomiformis*, most often found in upland areas on rock ledges and in crevices. Stems are matted with hairs near their bases and may grow to about 4cm long. Leaves are narrow and pointed, with white bases sheathing the stem. Fruit capsules are green and apple-shaped when young on stalks 1 to 3cm long, and are frequently produced in the summer.

Philonotis fontana (Hedw.) Brid. Common on wet ground around mountain springs and flushes, and occasionally by wet woodland rides. Bright yellowish-green plants are 1 to 10cm tall, matted at the base with short reddish-brown hairs. The short pointed leaves are triangular. Capsules are occasionally produced in summer. Male plants have small flower-like structures and crowns of radiating branches at their tips.

Orthotrichum anomalum Hedw. Frequently found on damp basic rocks and walls and rarely on trees. It forms small tufts, with each plant 0.5 to 5cm tall. The leaves are widely spread when moist but pressed to the stems when dry. Fruit capsules are common, produced in spring and summer on distinctive short red stalks. The capsules have hairy, pointed caps and lids which fall to expose a ring of teeth.

Amphidium mougeotii

Orthotrichum diaphanum Brid. Common as small cushions or tufts on fences, wood and rocks. Plants are about 1cm tall and have narrow leaves with short silvery hair points. Fruiting is common in winter and spring, with oval capsules produced on very short stalks; they have conical, grooved lids which fall when ripe to reveal a ring of teeth.

Orthotrichum lyellii Hook. & Tayl. Frequently found throughout Britain on trees in damp places. It forms looser tufts than the other *Orthotrichum* species shown. Stems are 1 to 4cm tall with long, narrow leaves which carry tiny gemmae, vegetative propagation structures. Fruiting capsules are very rare and grow in summer on tiny stalks so that they are almost buried by the rest of the plant.

Breutelia chrysocoma

Amphidium mougeotii (Hedw.) Schimp. Frequent in crevices of acidic rocks and cliffs in hilly districts of north and west Britain. Plants form yellowish cushions up to 8cm high and have long, narrow leaves which become twisted when dry. Resembles *Tortella tortuosa* but the leaves are narrower, not crisped or broken, with no strongly shining midrib when dry. Fruiting is very rare, with short-stalked pear-shaped capsules.

Ulota crispa (Hedw.) Brid. Common in upland districts of Britain on the branches of trees and shrubs, particularly on Ash, Hazel, Elder and Willow; uncommon in central and south-east England. Plants are 0.5 to 2cm tall, with narrow leaves tapering to long points. Fruit capsules are common throughout the year, on short stalks. They are covered with hairy caps which fall to expose the ripe furrowed capsules.

Breutelia chrysocoma (Hedw.) Lindb. Common in mountain districts on rock ledges near streams and damp soils on heaths and moors. Shoots are up to about 10cm tall, covered with thick brown hairs towards the base, and form loose tufts. Fruiting is rare, capsules produced on a yellow curved stalk. Male structures are in dark clusters at the shoot tips, surrounded by branches.

Ulota phyllantha Brid. Frequently found on rocks and trees just above the high-water mark on the west coasts of Britain, rare elsewhere. It forms yellowish tufts, reddish or brown at the base of stems. Plants are 0.5 to 2cm tall with long narrow leaves which become markedly twisted when dry. Fruit capsules are very rare and produced in autumn. Clusters of brown gemmae are borne on tips of upper leaves.

Hedwigia ciliata (Hedw.) P. Beauv. Locally common on acidic rock, walls and roofing slates, never on limestone; rare in south-east England and the Midlands. Plants are hoary and irregularly branched. The leaves are tapered to silvery hair points and become spreading when dry. Fruiting capsules are more or less stalkless and oblong, they are occasionally produced in spring.

Fontinalis antipyretica Hedw. Common on rocks or wood in rivers, ponds or lakes, usually submerged. Often known as Willow Moss, it grows to 80cm with dark green or dull olive keeled leaves, about 0.3 to 0.5cm long, in three rows. The name *antipyretica* means against fire, a reference to its use in protection of houses in Lapland from fire. Fruit capsules are rare, produced in spring among the leaves.

Neckera complanata (Hedw.) Hüb. Common on shaded tree trunks, rocks and walls, forming shiny yellowish tufts or patches. The shoots are flattened, branched in one plane and up to 5cm long. Leaves are oblong with tiny short points and are not wrinkled as in *N. crispa*. Fruit capsules are only occasionally produced in spring on short yellow stalks; they are orange-brown and oval in outline.

Neckera crispa Hedw. Common on limestone rocks, chalk grassland and sometimes on tree bases, but rare on lime-free substrates. It forms loose straggly patches with branched stems, 4 to 20cm long, strongly flattened and sometimes curling upwards at the tips. The leaves are oval and strongly waved crosswise. Fruit capsules are rare, produced in the spring on very short curved stalks, almost hidden among the leaves.

Thamnobryum alopecurum (Hedw.). Nieuwl., synonym *Thamnium alopecurum* (Hedw.) Br. Eur. Common on damp, shady rocks and trees. Similar to *Climacium dendroides*, but dark green with flatter fronds. Upright stems, about 3 to 4cm tall, have clusters of branches at the top. Stem leaves are broad and triangular; branch leaves are oblong with pointed, toothed tips. Fruit capsules are not common and produced in winter or spring on short stalks.

Climacium dendroides

Thuidium tamariscinum

Climacium dendroides (Hedw.) Web. & Mohr.
Found throughout Britain on damp ground in
woodland, grassland and dune slacks.
Branching leafless stems run along the ground
and give rise to erect stems 2 to 3cm tall with
branches crowded at the apex in a tree-like
manner (dendroid). Stem leaves are long, with
toothed tips and branch leaves are shorter with
hooded tips. Fruit capsules are very rare,
produced in winter on long curved stalks.

Anomodon viticulosus (Hedw.) Hook. & Tayl.
Common on rocks, walls, trees and fences in
limestone or chalk districts, rare elsewhere.
Leafless, root-like creeping stems give rise to
sparsely branched leafy shoots which are 2 to
12cm long. When moist the long round-tipped
leaves spread outwards, when dry they are
strongly curled. Fruiting is rare, capsules
produced in winter on long stalks.

Thuidium tamariscinum (Hedw.) Br. Eur.
Common throughout Britain on damp ground,
trees, rotting wood and rocks in woods and
other shady places. The bright green or golden
feathery stems form thick mats or tufts. Stems
are dark green or almost black with tiny
triangular leaves and regularly branched three
times. Fruit capsules are very rare but may be
found in spring in the damper west and north
of Britain.

Cratoneuron commutatum var. *commutatum*

Cratoneuron commutatum var. *falcatum*

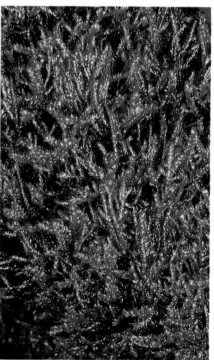

Cratoneuron commutatum (Hedw.) Roth var. *commutatum*. Common on wet basic rocks and in flushes in mountain regions and in fens and dune slacks in the lowlands. The bright yellowish-green stems are regularly branched and the long triangular leaves are curled in one direction giving an appearance which has been likened to an ostrich plume. Fruit capsules are curved and rare, produced in the spring.

Cratoneuron commutatum (Hedw.) Roth var. *falcatum* (Brid.) Monk. Common in basic areas on flushes, by mountain streams, fens and dune slacks. Plants look quite different to *C. commutatum* var. *commutatum* being stouter and only sparsely and irregularly branched. Leaves are narrower. Fruit capsules are rare, produced in spring.

Heterocladium heteropterum (Bruch ex Schwaegr.) Br. Eur. Common in upland areas of Britain on damp, shady rocks or soil by streams and in damp woodlands. Trailing matted stems are deep green and unevenly branched, the branches often pointing in one direction. Stem leaves are oval and pointed; branch leaves smaller and broader. Fruit capsules are very rare and produced in spring on purplish stalks.

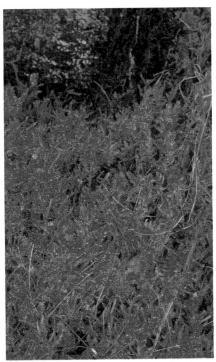

Amblystegium riparium (Hedw.) Br. Eur., synonym *Lepodictyum riparium* (Hedw.) Warnst. Frequent in lowland areas on rocks, wood or soil near streams and pools, and among plant litter in fens and marshes. Sparsely branched stems form loose straggly mats. Narrowly triangular, widely spreading leaves are larger than on *A. serpens* and taper to fine points. Curved, inclined fruit capsules are frequently produced in spring and summer.

Amblystegium serpens (Hedw.) Br. Eur. Common on wet shady rocks, soil, tree bases, rotting wood and walls. Slender branches grow from a network of stems and form delicate low tufts. The leaves are minute and not widely spreading. Fruit capsules are common, produced in spring through till autumn on red stalks, held horizontally until ripe when they become erect. Their whitish caps are conspicuous when young.

Drepanocladus uncinatus

Drepanocladus fluitans (Hedw.) Warnst. Found on peaty or acid marshes and bogs or submerged in shallow pools, usually at low altitudes. Soft, glossy, loosely branched plants up to 15cm long. Leaves are tapered to a toothed tip and are slightly curved. At shoot tips the leaves all curl in one direction. Fruit capsules are curved and produced on stalks 3 to 7cm long. They are rare and usually found in summer and autumn.

Drepanocladus revolvens (Sw.) Warnst. Most common in the north and west of Britain in peaty pools, bogs and flushes and on shaded wet rocks and cliff ledges. Orange or reddish tinged, loosely branched stems are up to 10cm long. Densely set leaves are strongly curled in one direction almost forming complete rings. Cylindrical, long-stalked fruit capsules are rare and produced in the summer.

Drepanocladus uncinatus (Hedw.) Warnst. Frequently found in mountain regions on rocks or plant litter by streams, in woods and on cliffs, and sometimes on trees, logs and soil. Stems are up to 10cm long covered with leaves strongly curved in one direction. Branching is more regular than most other *Drepanocladus* species. Curved, cylindrical, pale orange fruit capsules are common in the spring.

Scorpidium scorpioides

Calliergon cuspidatum

Calliergon stramineum (Brid.) Kindb., synonym
Acrocladium stramineum (Brid.) Rich. & Wall.
Frequent in most of Britain growing among
Sphagnum or other mosses or as a small tuft in
bogs, marshes, flushes and by streams or
pools. The slender, pale, loosely branched
plants lie on the ground or are slightly raised
and reach a length of about 15cm. Round-
tipped leaves are concave and clasp the stem.
Fruit capsules are curved, but rarely seen.

Scorpidium scorpioides (Hedw.) Limpr.
Common in the north and west of Britain on
wet peat usually on base-rich sites such as
flushes and by pools. The thick flaccid shoots
grow to 15cm or more and are usually purplish
or brownish. Leaves are oval, concave,
irregularly wrinkled, tapered to short points
and curve in one direction. Curved fruit
capsules are produced in spring and summer,
but are rare.

Calliergon cuspidatum (Hedw.) Kindb.,
synonym Acrocladium cuspidatum (Hedw.)
Lindb. Frequently found on chalk grassland
and wet boggy places, fens and damp parts of
sand dunes and often in lawns. Regularly
branched stems are up to 12cm. Yellowish
leaves are closely pressed together when young,
forming sharply pointed shoot tips. Fruit
capsules are occasionally produced in spring,
curved cylinders on long reddish stalks.

Homalothecium sericeum (Hedw.) Dr. Eur.,
synonym Camptothecium sericeum (Hedw.)
Kindb. Common on rocks, walls, hard ground
and trees. It forms thick silky mats, often
golden or yellow tinged, with regular close
branching curling upwards when dry. Leaves
are narrowly triangular and finely pointed.
Fruit capsules are erect and narrowly cone-
shaped on a purplish stalk, occasionally
produced in winter.

Homalothecium sericeum

Isothecium myosuroides

Brachythecium rivulare

Isothecium myurum Brid. Frequent throughout Britain, but more common in the south than *I. myosuroides*. It grows in dense, yellowish patches on damp tree bases, rocks and stumps. Stems are 2 to 3cm, densely branched in the upper part, the branches often curving in the same direction. Leaves are concave, shortly pointed and minutely toothed. Reddish brown, erect, cylindrical fruit capsules may be frequently produced in autumn and winter.

Isothecium myosuroides Brid. Common in the west of Britain on rocks, trees, logs and branches in damp shady places, especially woodland. Branched creeping stems give rise to secondary erect or procumbent, irregularly branched stems. Leaves on the upright stems are less concave than in *I. myurum*, taper to a point and have toothed edges. Fruit capsules are frequently produced in winter and are slightly curved.

Brachythecium rivulare Br. Eur. Common on flushes on mountainsides, on rocks and wood in and near streams and in wet woodland. Creeping branched shoots are up to 12cm long, bright yellowish-green or pale green, with crowded, pointed branches. Leaves are broad, pointed and minutely toothed. Fruiting is uncommon, inclined, swollen capsules produced on rough stalks in autumn through to spring.

Brachythecium plumosum

Brachythecium rutabulum

Brachythecium plumosum (Hedw.) Br. Eur.
Found in mountain districts on wet rocks by
lakes and fast-moving streams, growing in mats
or in scattered tufts. The more or less upright
branches are silky and tinged brownish
golden. Leaves are concave, minutely toothed,
and slightly curved, all pointing in one
direction. Fruit capsules have stalks smooth
below and are frequently found in winter.

Brachythecium rutabulum (Hedw.) Br. Eur.
Abundant on rocks, wood, trees and turf by
streams, rivers, roads, in lawns, gardens and
woodland. The glossy, golden or pale green
plants are much branched and form large tufts
or straggle through grass or other mosses.
Leaves are oval, sharply pointed and have
minutely toothed edges. Fruiting is common,
inclined capsules being produced on rough
stalks in autumn, winter and spring.

Cirriphyllum piliferum (Hedw.) Grout.
Common in lowland Britain in damp shaded
grassy places on basic soils, such as chalk or
heavy clay. It forms loose mats of regularly
branched stems up to 15cm long. Shoot tips
are pointed and the broad concave leaves have
distinctive long silvery hair-like tips. Fruiting
is rare, with curved horizontal capsules
produced on reddish, rough stalks in autumn
and winter.

Rhynchostegium confertum

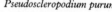

Pseudoscleropodium purum

Rhynchostegium confertum (Dicks.) Br. Eur., synonym *Eurhynchium confertum* (Dicks.) Milde. Common in lowland areas on soil, rocks and walls in woodland or other shady places. Irregularly branched stems form straggly light green tufts. Leaves are oval, minutely toothed with tapered tips. Fruiting is common in winter, the horizontal beaked capsules on smooth stalks distinguishing this species from *Brachythecium velutinum*.

Pseudoscleropodium purum (Hedw.) Fleisch. Common throughout Britain in grassland or on heaths and woodland clearings. Plants are up to 15cm long, regularly branched, the stems and branches with blunt rounded tips. Stems are pale, not red as in *Pleurozium schreberi*. The leaves are densely set and overlapping; they are broad and concave with a minute protruding tip. Fruit capsules are rare.

Eurynchium praelongum (Hedw.) Br. Eur. Common on tree bases, banks, stream and ditch sides in damp, shady places. The main stems are up to 12cm long and regularly branched. Leaves are heart-shaped on the main stems, toothed and sharply narrowed to recurved points; those on the branches are narrower than on the stem, and lance-shaped. Curved fruit capsules have long beaks and rough stalks, occasionally produced in winter.

Eurynchium praelongum

Plagiothecium nemorale

Plagiothecium undulatum

Eurynchium striatum (Hedw.) Schimp.
Common on calcareous soils, among grass or
on rocks and banks, usually in shaded places,
forming loose mats. The long stout stems are
irregularly branched. Leaves are triangular and
spreading with longitudinal folds. Fruiting is
occasional, with reddish-brown capsules
produced on long stalks in autumn and winter.

Plagiothecium denticulatum (Hedw.) Br. Eur.
Common in woodlands, marshes and shaded
rock ledges, on rotting wood or soil covered
rocks. The flattened shoots are bright green
with broad, oval pointed leaves and form shiny
patches. Fruiting is common, the slightly
inclined capsules carried on red stalks and
produced in spring and summer.

Plagiothecium nemorale (Mitt.) Jaeg., synonym
P. sylvaticum auct. Frequently found in
lowland districts, forming patches on soil in
woodland, hedge banks and by streams. The
branched plants have flattened shoots but are
dull dark green rather than glossy and pale as
most other *Plagiothecium* species. Leaves are
broad and shrivel noticeably when dry. Fruit
capsules are curved, inclined and occasionally
produced in summer.

Plagiothecium undulatum (Hedw.) Br. Eur.
Common in woodland, hedgebanks, heaths and
moors, particularly in the north and west of
Britain, but never on calcareous soil. The pale
whitish-green plants have broad, flattened
branches, larger than *P. denticulatum* and with
waved leaves. Fruiting capsules are not
common; they are long and curved and
produced in summer on orange stalks.

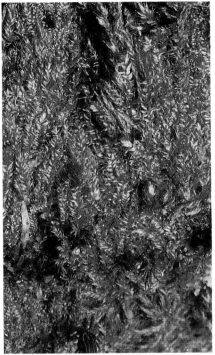

Hypnum cupressiforme

Hypnum jutlandicum

Isopterygium elegans (Brid.) Lindb. Common on sandy or peaty soils or acid rocks in woodland or other shaded place, never on calcareous substrates. It grows in flat silky mats and narrow leaves taper to a point. Fruiting is very rare; inclined capsules produced in spring. More common are clusters of thread-like, almost leafless shoots in leaf-axils, which are a means of vegetative reproduction.

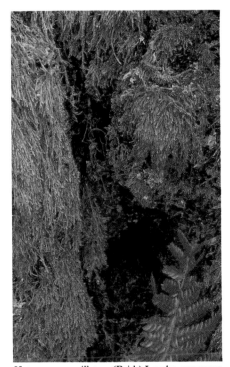

Hypnum mammillatum (Brid.) Loeske, synonym H. cupressiforme var. filiforme Brid. Frequently found on tree trunks, logs, rocks and walls. It differs from H. cupressiforme in having longer, narrower and less branched stems which form a thick hanging tassel. The leaves are similar but much smaller. Fruit capsules are produced in autumn and may be common. They are erect or slightly inclined and have a rounded lid with a small point.

Hypnum cupressiforme Hedw. Common on rocks, walls, tree bases, wood and soil, particularly in acidic areas. It grows in dense mats of regularly branched stems, with concave overlapping leaves not unlike those of a Cypress (Cupressus) tree. The leaves taper to long points curved downwards in the same direction. Fruiting may be frequent in autumn and winter, slightly curved short cylindrical capsules on red stalks.

Hypnum jutlandicum Holmen & Warncke, synonym H. cupressiforme var. ericetorum Br. Eur. Common on heaths and moors and on the floor of coniferous woods, never on calcareous soil. The loose pale mats of regularly branched stems are not closely attached to the ground. The leaves are less crowded than on H. cupressiforme and strongly curved to one side. Fruiting is rare, curved capsules produced in winter and spring.

Ptilium cristacastrensis

Ctenidium molluscum (Hedw.) Mitt. Common in basic habitats such as calcareous grassland, cliffs and fens. The plants are usually golden or bronze, may form thick mats and are regularly and closely branched in a feather shape. Leaves have heart-shaped bases and tapered, curved tips pointing in one direction. Inclined fruit capsules have purple stalks and conical lids, they are rare, produced in winter.

Hyocomium armoricum (Brid.) Wijk & Marg., synonym *H. flagellare* Br. Eur. Common in the north and west of Britain on rocks and tree roots by mountain streams and waterfalls. Stems are regularly branched, up to about 5cm long, and form loose bright green or golden-tinged mats. Stem leaves are toothed and sharply pointed; branch leaves smaller and unpointed. Fruiting is rare, with capsules produced on rough, purple stalks in winter.

Ptilium cristacastrensis (Hedw.) De Not. Uncommon, found in leaf litter in coniferous woods in the north of Scotland and rarely in north Wales. The plants are bright green or tinged golden. Branching is crowded and very regular. Leaves are curled almost in a circle all in one direction. Fruiting is rare, curved capsules with short pointed lids produced in autumn.

Hylocomium splendens (Hedw.) Br. Eur. Common on soil in woodland, on heaths, moors, roadside and sand dunes forming glossy yellowish or brownish carpets. The red stems are branched regularly, then branched again (bipinnate), which distinguishes it from *Pleurozium schreberi*. Leaves are transparent, oval, toothed and pointed. Fruit capsules are produced in spring and are very rare.

Rhytidiadelphus loreus (Hedw.) Warnst. Common in the north and west of Britain on logs and acid soil in woodland, rock ledges and heaths. Stems are red and regularly branched and covered with narrow triangular leaves, with tapered points which curve in one direction. Fruit capsules are horizontal with a conical or pointed lid; they are only occasionally produced in winter.

Rhytidiadelphus squarrosus   *Rhytidiadelphus triquetrus*   *Pleurozium schreberi*

Rhytidiadelphus squarrosus (Hedw.) Warnst.
Common on damp turf and banks in woodland,
by streams and in marshes and often in lawns.
It has smaller, more slender stems than
R. triquetrus, but is similarly branched and
forms dense tufts or mats. The leaves are
triangular with long tapered points which
curve back on themselves. Fruiting is very rare,
with capsules produced in winter.

Rhytidiadelphus triquetrus (Hedw.) Warnst.
Common among grass or in patches on
moorland, mountain sides, sand dunes and
woodland but not on very acid soils. The
sturdy, irregularly branched stems may be up
to 20cm long. The stems are reddish and the
pale leaves are triangular, pointed and curve
outwards. Fruit capsules are produced in
winter but are rarely found.

Pleurozium schreberi (Brid.) Mitt. Common in
dry places on heaths, moors, mountain slopes,
sand dunes and scree, never on calcareous
ground. It grows in thick mats with stiff,
bright red stems, regularly branched in one
plane. Leaves are oval with slightly inrolled
edges, those on the stem twice the size of
those on the branches. Fruiting is rare, capsules
occasionally produced in autumn and winter.

Sphagnum capillifolium

Sphagnum auriculatum var. *auriculatum*

Sphagnum auriculatum var. *inundatum*

Sphagnum capillifolium (Ehrh.) Hedw., synonyms *S. rubellum* Wils., *S. nemoreum* Scop. Most commonly found in the north and west on bogs, moors and marshes, often forming a carpet under heather or on top of hummocks. Shoots grow to about 15cm, usually crimson, pinkish or green, tinged with pink. Stems are red or green with triangular leaves. Branch leaves are smaller and narrower. Fruit capsules are occasionally produced in summer.

Sphagnum auriculatum Schimp. var. *auriculatum*. Common throughout Britain in damp woods, moors, bog pools and acid flushes. It grows in large masses, with shoots up to about 20cm often tinged orange or reddish-brown. Stems are dark brown or black. Branches are long and pointed and may be curved. Stem leaves have rounded tips and branch leaves are oval and pointed. Fruit capsules are occasionally produced in the summer.

Sphagnum auriculatum Schimp. var *inundatum* (Russ.) M. O. Hill, synonym *S. subsecundum* var. *inundatum* (Russ.) C. Jens. Found throughout Britain forming extensive patches in flushes, fens, marshes and damp hollows on heathland. Plants are similar to *S. auriculatum* var. *auriculatum*, with dark stems, but it is more slender and has more pronounced hanging branches. Fruit capsules are produced in summer and are not common.

Sphagnum palustre

Sphagnum papillosum

Sphagnum palustre L. Common and widespread by streams in wet woodland and moorland. One of the best distinguishing features is its whitish-green colour, sometimes tinged pinkish or bright green. It is also thick and robust with swollen, tapering mature branches. Stems are up to 25cm long. Stem leaves have wide round tips and branch leaves are larger with hooded tips. Fruit capsules are frequent, produced in early summer.

Sphagnum papillosum Linb. Common throughout Britain on moors and bogs, at the base of hummocks. Closely related to *S. palustre* but grows in wetter, more acid habitats and forms yellowish green or ochre tussocks. Plants are up to about 25cm long with short blunt branches. Stem leaves are broadest at the tip with jagged edges, branch leaves are concave and rounded. Fruit capsules are occasionally produced in summer.

Sphagnum magellanicum Brid. Found throughout Britain, though rare in the south and east of England, on acid bogs. It is closely related to *S. palustre* and *S. papillosum*, but has a red stem and the whole tussock is usually tinged dark wine or red coloured. Fruit capsules are rare and produced in summer.

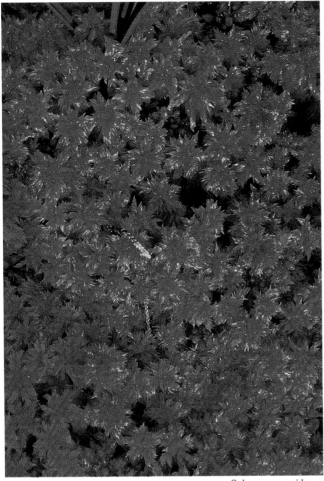

Sphagnum cuspidatum

Sphagnum subnitens

Sphagnum cuspidatum Hoffm. Most common in the north and west of Britain, on acid bogs and moors, or growing as an aquatic in pools and lakes. Green or yellowish land forms grow to 15cm; the pale, submerged forms may be twice as long and recognized by their floppy 'drowned cat' appearance. Stems are green, stem leaves triangular, and branch leaves long, narrow and wavy when dry. Fruit capsules are not common, produced in the summer.

Sphagnum subnitens Russ. & Warnst., synonym *S. plumulosum* Röll. Common in blanket bogs and moorland in the north and west and wet heaths in the south. Plants are up to 20cm long and may be green, dull red or brown; but not bright red as in *S. capillifolium*. Dry leaves have a distinctive metallic sheen. Branch and stem leaves have pointed tips, the latter are triangular and the former, oval. Fruit capsules are common and may be found in the summer.

Sphagnum compactum DC. Common on blanket bogs, damp heaths and moors, especially after burning. It grows in compact orange-tinted or yellowish tussocks with shoots up to 10cm long. The branches are short, thick and blunt-tipped, the upper ones pointing upwards. Stem leaves are tiny and triangular; branch leaves larger with edges curled inwards on the branches. Fruit capsules are frequently produced in spring.

Marchantia polymorpha

Conocephalum conicum

Lunularia cruciata

Marchantia polymorpha L. Common throughout Britain on moors and heaths particularly after burning, also found in flower pots and in greenhouses. The broad, branched plants are dark green and carry clusters of vegetative propagation structures (gemmae) in complete cups. Male and female structures are produced in spring and summer on stalks, the male parts flat and disc like, the female parts with about nine spreading rays.

Conocephalum conicum (L.) Underw. Common on damp shaded rocks by ditches, streams, on walls and mountain ledges. The plants are about 1 to 1.5cm broad and up to 20cm long, forming flat lush carpets. They are marked with a hexagonal pattern, each hexagon containing a distinct pore. Male structures are in purplish bumps near branch tips. Fruit capsules are infrequent, produced in cone-shaped structures on thin stalks underneath the cone.

Lunularia cruciata (L.) Dum. Common in flower pots and gardens, sometimes considered an annoying weed; also found by streams and in woodland. Smaller than *Conocephalum conicum*, 1.5 to 2.5cm long and 0.5 to 1cm broad. The surface is covered with pores and vegetative propagation structures (gemmae) in clusters, half surrounded by a crescent-shaped flap. Spores are very rarely produced.

Preissia quadrata

Riccardia pinguis

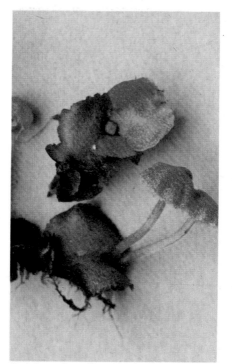

Preissia quadrata (Scop.) Nees. Frequent on mountain rock ledges, damp hollows of sand dunes and damp calcareous rocks, never on acid substrates, most common in the north and west of Britain. Paler green and smaller than *Marchantia polymorpha*, edged purplish-brown and lacking gemma-cups. Fruit capsules are frequent and formed on the undersides of four-sided umbrella-shaped structures. Male structures are flatter and on shorter stalks.

Riccardia pinguis (L.) Gray. Common in very wet habitats such as fen peat, flushes, and wet rocks. It is 2 to 3cm long and about 0.5cm broad, more delicate than *Pellia epiphylla*, with branches more or less at right angles. Fruit capsules are frequent, oval, dark green on long stalks; they break open into a cross shape when ripe. Male structures are on separate plants, embedded in the tips of side branches.

Riccia glauca L. Common on fields, gardens, banks and woodland rides and is most noticeable in autumn and winter. Its lobes are 0.1 to 0.3cm broad and overlap, spreading outwards in a circular pattern and 1cm across. Spores are produced in capsules which are embedded in the main part of the plant, as are the male reproductive structures.

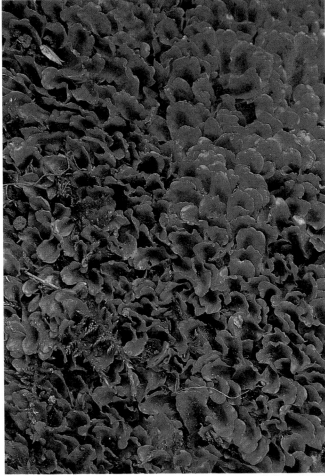

Pellia epiphylla

Tritomaria quinquedentata

Pellia epiphylla (L.) Corda. Common
throughout Britain on damp soil by ditches and
streams and on wet peat and rocks in moorland
and mountains. Plants are dull green about
0.8 to 1cm broad, with no surface markings.
Male structures are small, often reddish bumps
behind the females which produce round,
black spore capsules on long white stalks.
P. endiviifolia Dicks. is common in calcareous
districts, smaller and curved at the edges.

Tritomaria quinquedentata (Huds.) Buch.
Frequent on peat covered rocks and walls in
mountains. Stems are little branched and grow
to about 2.5cm long. Leaves are in two rows
and are distinctive being divided asymetrically
into three pointed lobes. Fruit capsules are
produced inside a pleated barrel-shaped sheath.
Vegetative propagation structures (gemmae)
are often produced in clusters on leaves near
shoot tips.

Lepidozia reptans (L.) Dum. Common on
rotting wood, peat or moist banks, sometimes
on sandstone or moorland; never on calcareous
substrates. It grows in delicate, green mats of
branched stems, 0.5 to 2cm long. These have
two rows of three- or four-lobed leaves and a
third row of similar, but smaller, underleaves.
Oblong cylindrical yellowish spore capsules are
produced within long tubular structures
narrowed to furrowed tips.

Nardia scalaris

Marsupella emarginata

Plagiochila asplenioides

Nardia scalaris (Schrad.) Gray. Common throughout Britain on sandy and gravelly soils on moors, mountains, heaths but not on limestone or chalk. Stems are 1 to 3cm long, almost unbranched, forming large patches of light yellowish-green or reddish-brown. Leaves are round, concave and closely pressed together in two rows. Underleaves are tiny, narrow and pointed. Spore capsules are produced inside pear-shaped structures and are not common.

Marsupella emarginata (Ehrh.) Dum. Common in mountain regions on siliceous rock ledges and banks, also found at lower altitudes. Stems are 1 to 4cm tall, forming brownish or reddish-brown patches. Leaves are in two rows, and are round in outline with indented tips. Fertile shoots have leaves more crowded and carry tubular structures containing the spore capsules.

Plagiochila asplenioides (L.) Dum. Common on damp shady rocks, soil and walls, particularly on limestone. Stems are little branched, about 2 to 10cm, upright and clustered together into lax tufts. Leaves are attached to the stem at an angle and are rounded with toothed edges. Spore capsules are oval, brown and produced inside tubular structures and when ripe emerge on long stalks.

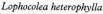

Lophocolea cuspidata

Lophocolea heterophylla

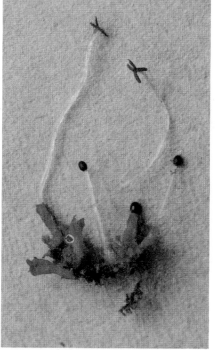

Lophocolea cuspidata (Nees) Limpr. Common on rotting logs, branches and stumps, sometimes on trees and grassy banks. Stems are 1 to 3cm long, in compact tufts. Leaves are crowded and have two pointed teeth. Underleaves are minute and deeply divided. Capsules are common, in long tubular structures with jagged tips.
L. bidentata (L.) Dum. Common and similar with less symetrical, lobed leaves.

Lophocolea heterophylla (Schrad.) Dum. Common on decaying stumps and logs, occasionally found on sandstone. Branched stems are 1 to 2cm long and have two rows of leaves some with two pointed teeth, some with two blunt lobes and some untoothed. There is a third row of deeply cut, inconspicuous underleaves. In spring numerous black capsules on white stalks emerge from tubular sheaths. When ripe they break open into cross-shapes.

Lophozia ventricosa (Dicks) Dum. Common on sandy and peaty soils and on rotting wood, always on acid substrates. Stems are 1 to 3cm long, crowded together in bright green patches. Leaves are shallowly divided into two lobes and there are no underleaves. Fruit capsules are produced inside an oval open-topped structure, but more common are bright green clusters of vegetative propagation structures (gemmae) on leaves at shoot tips.

Cephalozia biscuspidata (L.) Dum. Common in damp acid habitats on banks, woodland rides, rotting wood and *Sphagnum* bogs often growing through moss. Stems are 0.5 to 2cm long with two rows of delicate leaves, each divided into two pointed lobes. Fruiting is common, with the spore capsules produced inside a long, whitish, tubular protective structure (perianth), which is surrounded by shorter two-lobed bracts.

Scapania nemorea (L.) Grolle. Common on damp shady soil or sometimes rotting wood in loose green or brown tinged patches. Stems are 1 to 6cm and little branched. Leaves are toothed and have two lobes, one large and rounded, the other smaller folded over it. Vegetative propagation structures (gemmae) are small, dark brown clusters on leaves at stem tips. Fruit capsules are produced in tubular sheaths with fringed open tops.

Pleurozia purpurea Lindb. Locally frequent on moorland peat and on mountain rock ledges in Scotland and Ireland, rare in northern England. It forms dark purplish red patches of little branched shoots up to 14cm in length. Leaves are in two rows and closely overlap. Each leaf has a large concave toothed lobe and a hood-shaped lobe which holds water and is thought to help provide nutrients by trapping tiny insects.

Porella platyphylla (L.) Lindb. Common in calcareous districts on shady banks, tree bases, old walls and rocks, especially in beech woods. The branched stems grow from 3 to 8cm long and form compact dark green or yellow-tinged patches. The side leaves have a large, rounded lobe, and a smaller narrow lobe, folded underneath. There is a row of large underleaves. Tubular structures containing fruit capsules are frequent.

Frullania dilatata (L.) Dum. Common on tree trunks, especially Elm, Ash and Elder, sometimes on shady rocks. Stems are branched, closely attached to the substrate and may be green or dull reddish-brown. Leaves have a large rounded upper lobe and a smaller helmet-shaped lobe underneath. Smaller underleaves with two-pointed lobes are closely pressed to the stem. Spore capsules are common in pear-shaped structures.

Frullania tamarisci (L.) Dum. Common on trees, rocks or on heather stems in the north and west of Britain, less frequent in the south and east. Larger than *F. dilatata*, with much branched reddish or purplish-brown stems. Leaves are in two rows, each divided into a larger round lobe and a smaller helmet-shaped lobe. The smaller stem leaves have two rounded lobes. Spore capsules are formed within a three-sided smooth tubular structure.

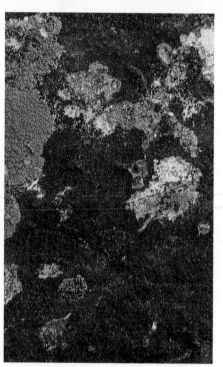

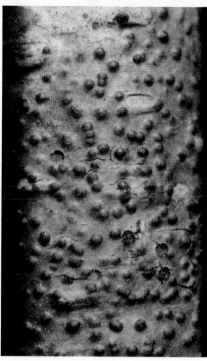

Lepraria incana (L.) Ach. Common in damp, shady places on trees, soil and rocks, but protected from the rain itself. It cannot grow in direct sunlight. It often grows in large patches, making a soft, thick, grey, completely powdery crust. No spores are produced.

Verrucaria maura Wahlenb. ex Ach. A maritime lichen which is abundant on rocks at the highwater mark. It forms a thin black crust covered with fine cracks. It could be mistaken for tar stains when covering large areas of rock. The photograph also shows *Caloplaca thallincola*, which is orange.

Pyrenula nitida (Weigel) Ach. Frequent in the wetter western parts of Britain on smooth-barked trees. It forms a smooth, waxy crust, greenish grey when damp and brownish when dry. Neighbouring colonies are divided by dark wavy thallus lines. The circular spore-producing discs are blackish and become domed with a central opening when mature.

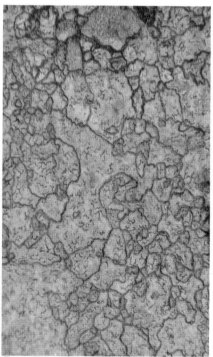

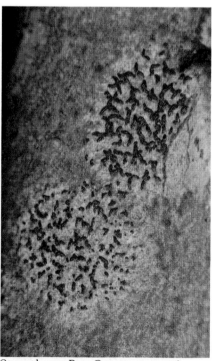

Enterographa crassa (DC.) Fée. Common in the south of Britain on shaded, hard-barked trees. It forms a thick greyish-green crust which is covered with a network of dark lines which look like boundaries on a map. Spores are produced in structures embedded in the crust, which are seen as dark spots or short lines near the wavy boundary lines.

Graphis scripta (L.) Ach. Common on tree bark throughout Britain, except in polluted areas. It forms a smooth or wrinkled grey crust with fruiting bodies forming dark curved lines scattered or forming straight parallel lines. *G. elegans* (Borrer. ex Sm.) Ach. Grows on trees and is more common in the south and west. The fruiting bodies form dark lines with furrowed edges; otherwise it looks similar to *G. scripta*.

Opegrapha atra Pers. Common on smooth-barked trees and fences and may be rather variable. It grows as thin pale grey patches covered with dark, straight, curved or branched lines (lirellae) which are the openings of the spore-producing structures and are usually smooth-edged and clustered towards the centre.

Baeomyces rufus (Huds.) Rebent. Found on peaty, sandy or gravelly soils, damp rocks in woods and on moors, especially common in hilly or mountain districts. It forms a soft greyish-green crust with stalked brown spore-producing bodies (apothecia) which look like tiny mushrooms.
B. roseus Pers. looks similar but has pink stalked apothecia arising from a whitish-grey granular crust. It grows on gravelly soil.

Icmadophila ericetorum (L.) Zahlbr. Found on damp peat and rotting wood; most common on Scottish moorland, and frequent on suitable habitats elsewhere, chiefly in the north. It grows as a soft crust, greyish-white when dry and greenish when damp, forming patches up to about 5cm across. Spore-producing discs are pink, marginate when young and unstalked, which distinguishes it from the similar looking *Baeomyces roseus*.

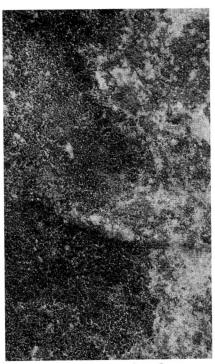

Placynthium nigrum (Huds.) Gray. Common on calcareous rocks and walls, usually on limestone. Its blackish patches are often irregular in shape and may be quite large. When closely examined it is seen to be made up of tiny scales or rounded granules on a thin blue-black layer which is often conspicuous at the edge of the lichen. Spore-producing structures are tiny glossy black discs.

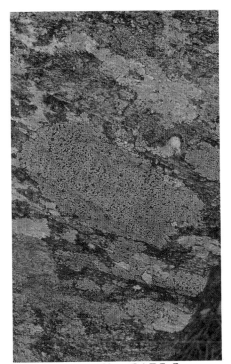

Rhizocarpon geographicum (L.) DC. Common on hard acid rocks and walls in upland areas. The crusted thallus is bright yellowish-green and forms highly conspicuous patches. The under layer is black and shows through cracks in the surface and as a thin black line round the edge. Colonies close together are separated by these black margins and look like countries on a map. Spore-producing structures are black and embedded in the crust.

Lecidea granulosa (Hoffm.) Ach. Common on rotting stumps and damp soil peat especially on heaths. It forms a whitish-grey granular crust which is often covered with greenish powdery structures which reproduce vegetatively. The spore-producing structures are also common and are convex discs, generally pinkish in colour with no margin.

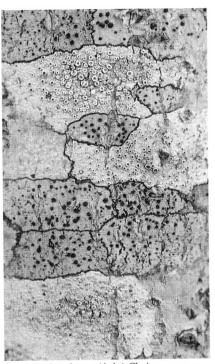

Lecidella elaeochroma (Ach.) Choisy, synonym *Lecidea limitata* (Scop.) Gray. Common on trees in less polluted areas, and sometimes on wood. It grows as a thin greenish-grey crust which is sometimes surrounded by a thin dark line. The spore-producing bodies are convex black discs.

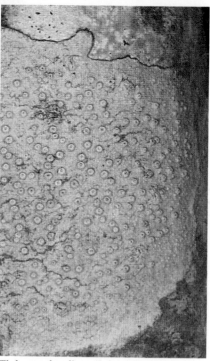

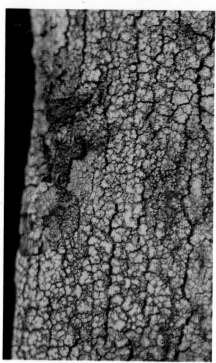

Lecidea lucida (Ach.) Ach. Common on damp siliceous rocks and brick walls in shaded situations. It forms vivid greenish-yellow powdery patches. Spore-producing structures are not common but are not easy to distinguish as they are minute and of the same colour as the rest of the colony.

Thelotrema lepadinum (Ach.) Ach. Common in the south and west of Britain on smooth-barked trees and sometimes on rocks. The pale, creamy-grey crust is thick, shiny and wrinkled. The spore-producing structures are embedded in the crust and form small wart-like lumps which develop a small dark hole in their centres when the spores are ripe.

Pertusaria amara (Ach.) Nyl. Common throughout Britain on trees and fences, and sometimes on mosses and siliceous walls. It grows in grey granular crusts and can be identified by its bitter taste, which is due to a high acid content. Sporing discs are very rare, reproduction being by whitish floury vegetative structures (soredia).

Pertusaria corallina (L.) Arnold. Common on siliceous rocks in upland districts. It forms a thick grey crust often surrounded by a narrow white line. Its surface is very rough and when examined with a hand-lens can be seen to be covered with tiny granular warts called isidia. Spore-producing structures are rare.

Pertusaria pertusa (L.) Tuck. Common throughout Britain on trees. It forms rough thick greenish-grey crusts which are commonly circular in outline. Spore-producing structures are buried in the crust, two or three together, causing a wart-like bump which opens to expose dark centres when the spores are ripe.

Cudbear Lichen or **Crottle** *Ochrolechia tartarea* (L.) Massal. Found in upland districts on siliceous rocks, tree-bases and mosses. It has been used, particularly in Scotland and Wales, as a source of crimson or purple dye which was extracted by seeping in urine. It forms thick grey crusts with a rough, warty surface and has concave pinkish discs with swollen wavy pale margins.

Crawfish Lichen or **Crab's Eye Lichen** or **Light Crottle** *Ochrolechia parella* (L.) Massal. Common on siliceous walls and rocks and sometimes on trees. This lichen was used as a source of red or orange dye. Its appearance is smoother than *O. tartarea*, forming a whitish-grey crust. Flesh-pink discs with swollen whitish margins are clustered in the centre. These gave it the names Crawfish and Crab's Eye Lichen.

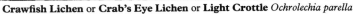

Crawfish Lichen or **Crab's Eye Lichen** or **Light Crottle** *Ochrolechia parella*

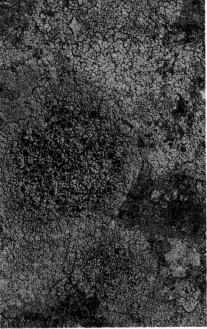

Black Shields *Lecanora atra* (Huds.) Ach. Common on siliceous rocks and walls, rarely on trees, particularly characteristic on rocks by the sea above the high-tide mark. It forms a thick pale grey crust which is cracked and warty. In the centre conspicuous spore-producing discs are formed; these are black with grey wavy margins.

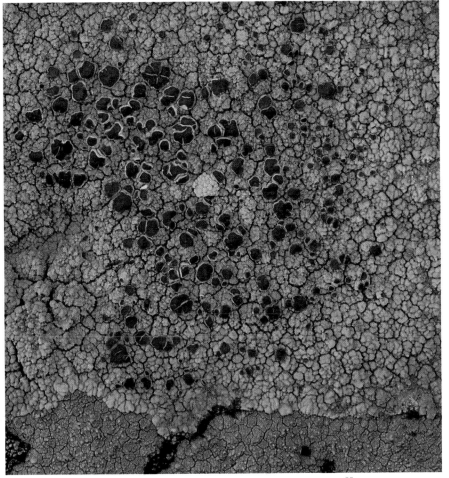

Haematomma ventosum

Haematomma ventosum (L.) Massal. Found on mountain siliceous rocks and boulders. It forms pale greenish or grey crusts with a warty surface and is conspicuous because of its large blood-red discs. These are common among members of this genus and give it its name from *haema*, Greek for blood.

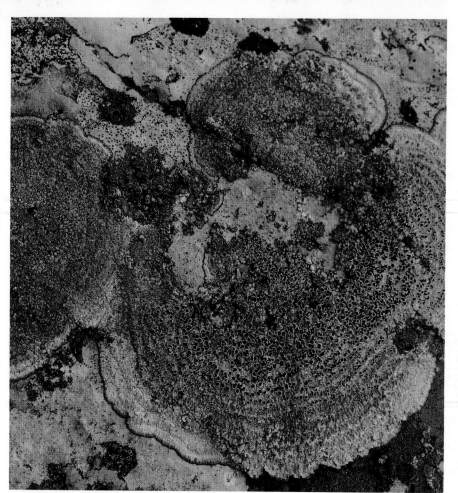

Aspicilia calcarea (L.) Mudd synonym
Lecanora calcarea (L.) Sommerf. Common on
calcareous rocks and limestone walls. It forms
an even, light grey crust with a white edge.
Spore-producing blackish discs are formed
inside the crust below the surface.

Aspicilia calcarea

Lecanora conizaeoides Nyl. ex Crombie.
Common on bark, wood and walls throughout
eastern England particularly in industrial and
urban areas. Generally absent from unpolluted
mountainous areas. It has a thick grey-green
granular-powdery cracked crust with pale
greenish discs with grey-green margins.

Lecanora chlarotera Nyl. Common on trees
where it forms a thin grey crust. Spore-
producing structures are disc shaped and
quite conspicuous. They are light brown with
smooth or wrinkled grey edges.

Lecanora chlarotera

Lecanora dispersa (Pers.) Sommerf. One of the commonest lichens in Britain, found on limestone rocks, walls, concrete and mortar and sometimes on trees. One of the few lichens which grows in city centres, it forms a white, grey or dark crust with clustered or scattered small, 0.5 to 1mm diameter, discs which are pale brown with whitish margins.

Lecanora dispersa

Mycoblastus sanguinarius (L.) Norman, synonym *Lecidea sanguinaria* (L.) Ach. Found commonly in upland areas on coniferous and deciduous trees, particularly birch. It forms a rough, light grey crust with a warted texture. The spore-producing structures are convex black discs 1 to 4mm in diameter. Where the surface is rubbed off a bright red layer shows through, a characteristic of the species.

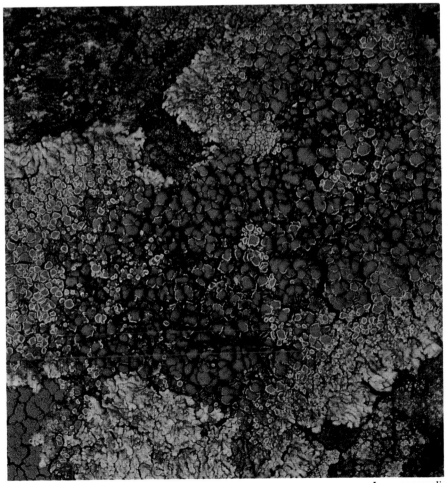

Lecanora muralis

Lecanora muralis (Schreber) Rabenh. Common on walls, concrete, cement, asbestos-cement roofs and rocks especially in nutrient-rich habitats. It forms a yellowish-brown crust with lobed edges. Spore-producing discs are usually present and clustered in the centre, pale brown in colour with wavy margins.

Candelariella aurella (Hoffm.) Zahlbr. Common on rocks and walls, especially on calcareous substrates such as cement and mortar, particularly in towns. Similar to *C. vitellina* but it grows in small scattered patches of poorly developed crust. (It is shown here mixed with *Lecanora dispersa*.) Spore-producing discs are very small but are abundant.

Candelariella vitellina (Hoffm.) Müll. Arg. Common on siliceous rocks, walls and fences, particularly where enriched by animal or bird droppings. It grows in large grainy thin crusts and is yellowish in colour. Spore-producing discs are mustard yellow, becoming darker with age and have well defined borders.

Caloplaca ferruginea (Huds.) Th. Fr. Common on siliceous rocks, walls and trees in unpolluted areas and by the sea well above the high-tide mark. The body of this lichen forms a grey, cracked and rather thin crust. It is the bright rust-reddish coloured spore-producing discs, produced in great quantity, which draw attention to the colonies.

Caloplaca heppiana (Müll. Arg.) Zahlbr. Common on limestone, occasionally on concrete and mortar. The orange closely compressed colonies form rosette shapes with lobed edges, each lobe slightly convex and swollen. In the centre are orange-bordered discs.
C. aurantia (Pers.) Hellbom grows in similar habitats. It is brighter orange with flattened lobes and becomes darker in the centre with age, taking on a zoned appearance.

Caloplaca marina (Wedd.) Zahlbr. Common on rocks by the sea just above high-tide mark. It does not form distinct lobed rosettes as in *C. heppiana*, but is often found as a scattered orange crust. Spore-producing discs are common, with distinct margins in the early stages. The photograph shows *C. marina* with *Verrucaria maura* and *Lichina confinis*.

Caloplaca thallincola (Wedd.) Du Rietz. Common on rocks by the sea just above high-water mark in open, unshaded situations. Very similar to *C. heppiana* with similar orange convex lobes, but these form parallel ridges in this species. Orange spore-producing discs with well defined borders are common in the centres of the rosettes.

Buellia canescens (Dickson) de Not. Common on rocks and walls and also frequently found on trees, especially in slightly shaded habitats rich in nutrients. It grows in circular patches which are pale grey when dry and pale green when wet; the lichen is closely compressed and the outside edge is lobed. Spore-producing discs are black with pale edges but are rare. Vegetative propagation structures are more frequent in the form of a whitish powder.

Buellia canescens

Solenopsora candicans (Dickson) Steiner. Frequent in England and Wales on limestone. It forms white or pale grey circular crusts with lobed edges and a cracked centre with black spore-producing discs with white margins when young.

Lecidea scalaris (Ach.) Ach. Common on decayed wood on old trees and fences and sometimes on rocks and walls. It grows as crowded patches of pale greenish overlapping scales. Vegetative reproductive structures are produced on the underside of these scales looking whitish-grey and powdery. Spore-producing structures are not common, but most frequently found in Scotland; they are black and formed on the upper surface.

Lecidea scalaris

Xanthoria parietina

Xanthoria parietina (L.) Th. Fr. Very common everywhere except in mountain regions. It grows on rocks, walls, roofs and trees especially where nitrogen enriched by bird or animal droppings, and near the sea. The circular leafy patches are usually bright yellow-orange but may sometimes be greenish-grey in shady places. Spore-producing bodies are present in quantity and have darker orange discs.

Xanthoria aureola (Ach.) Erichsen. Found on rocks and walls, especially on calcareous substrates such as cement and mortar. Common in the east of England. It forms yellowish-orange crusts, similar to *X. parietina* but is covered with rod-shaped growths (isidia). Large orange spore-producing discs may also be produced but are scattered.

Xanthoria aureola

Normandina pulchella (Borrer) Nyl. Fairly common in the west of Britain. Grows on other lichens (*Parmelia* and *Parmeliella*) and mosses on tree trunks and sometimes on walls and rock. The thallus is blue-green to pale grey, made up of 1 to 2mm diameter scales which may be scattered or grouped. The edges are raised and the surface may sometimes be covered by powdery vegetative structures. The underside is tomentose.

Squamarina crassa (Huds.) Poelt. Common in the south and west of Britain on soil in crevices of limestone rock. It has a squamulose thallus; that is, made up of small scales. These are dark green when damp and brownish-green when they dry out and sometimes have a bluish powder towards the edges. They are dark brown underneath and may have reddish spore-producing discs on the upper surface.

Squamarina crassa

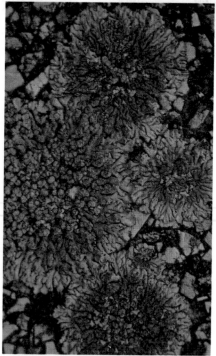

Physcia adscendens (Fr.) H. Olivier. Common on trees, rocks and walls, growing in small, grey patches loosely attached to its substrate. The narrowly lobed edges are turned upwards at their tips to expand into helmet shapes. Vegetative reproductive structures (soralia) are produced in powdery clusters on the undersides of the hooded lobes. Spore-producing discs are brownish-black with pale grey margins and are not common.

Physcia caesia (Hoffm.) Fürnrohr. Common on rocks and walls especially where enriched by bird or animal droppings. It forms bluish-grey lobed patches, pale brown or whitish underneath, with dark root-like structures. Round white or grey vegetative structures (soralia) are produced on the upper surface.

Anaptychia fusca (Huds.) Vainio. Common on rocks and sometimes trees or soil, by the sea above the high-tide mark, and may also be found on siliceous rocks inland in western districts. It forms thick dark brown foliose (leafy) cushions which are loosely attached to the rock. It may be green in colour when wet and has a duller surface than similar *Parmelia* species. Spores are produced in black discs with pale notched margins in the centre of the plant.

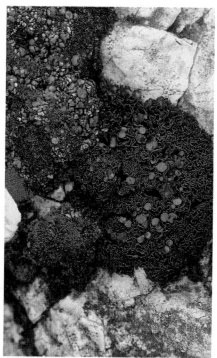

Collema auriculatum Hoffm. Found most commonly in the south and west on calcareous rocks. The lobed plants are about 3cm across and are dark brownish-green and fleshy when wet, thinner and dark with a bluish tinge when dry. The centre is covered with round blobs, which are known as isidia. Spore-producing structures are disc shaped.

Collema crispum (Huds.) Weber. Common on calcareous rocks, walls and old mortar, especially in shaded places. It is greenish-brown or almost black and forms rounded more or less overlapping lobes densely packed together. Spore-producing discs have granular or wavy edges.

Collema furfuraceum (Arnold) Du Rietz. Common in the north and west of Britain on old trees and sometimes on rocks. It is dark greenish or brownish-black, each plant about 2 to 6cm across, grouped together to form large patches. The lobes are ridged and there are tiny rod-shaped growths (isidia) in places. Spore-producing structures are very rare.

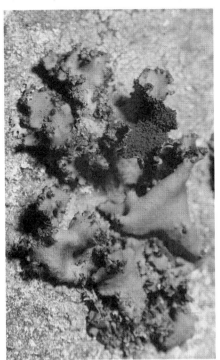

Leptogium burgessii (L.) Mont. Most common in the north and west of Britain on moss-covered trees, less often on rocks. It has a thick gelatinous texture when wet and becomes thin and brittle and paler in colour when dry. The lobes have wavy edges, the underside with short hairs. The reddish-brown discs are common and surrounded by a ring of tiny scales.

Umbilicaria polyrrhiza (L) Fr. Found on siliceous rocks and walls of upland areas of England, Wales and Scotland, especially the latter. It forms a thick lobed thallus, smooth, glossy chestnut-coloured above and covered below with black branched hairs (rhizinae) which project around the edge. Spores are rarely produced but appear in black discs on the upper surface.

Rock Tripe *Umbilicaria pistulata* (L.) Hoffm. Frequent in the west of Britain particularly in hilly areas on siliceous rocks in sunny situations. It may be eaten and is prepared by boiling then frying in oatmeal. Also used as a source of dye for red or purple. It forms circular patches, 3 to 6cm across, greenish-brown when wet and blackish when dry, covered with oval blister-like swellings.

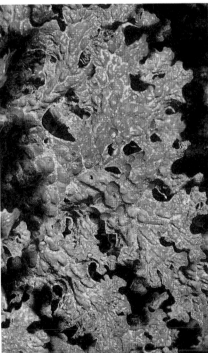

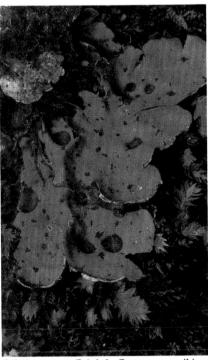

Parmeliella plumbea (Lightf.) Vainio. Common in damp western districts on moss-covered trees and rocks. The bluish-grey patches have radiating lines and concentric zones near the edges. Spore-producing structures are brown discs with pale brown margins. The centre of the plant may be rough or warty but never produces rod-shaped growths (isidia). *P. atlantica* Degel. is similar but the centre is covered with isidia.

Tree Lungwort *Lobaria pulmonaria* (L.) Hoffm. Found in western districts on trees and rocks. Large plants, 8 to 18cm long, are loosely attached to the substrate. Green and leathery when wet, they become pale and papery when dry; the upper surface has rounded depressions with granules on the ridges. Spore-producing structures are uncommon, but are shown in the photograph as reddish-brown discs.

Solorina saccata (L.) Ach. Common on soil in cracks between limestone rocks and sometimes on old limestone walls. It forms leaf-like patches which are bright green when damp, pale brown, often with a powdery bloom, when dry. Spore-producing discs are dark brown and slightly depressed, nearly always present. The lower surface is downy, pale brown to white.

Dog Lichen *Peltigera canina* (L.) Willd. Common throughout Britain on walls, rocks and soil amongst grasses in woods, lawns and sand dunes. It forms large lobed patches often 10cm across; thick, downy and dull brown when wet and pale grey when dry. The underside is white, downy and covered with white root-like growths. Spore-producing structures are not shown in the photograph: they are reddish-brown discs on the edges of lobes.

Dog Lichen *Peltigera canina*

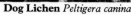

Peltigera polydactyla (Necker) Hoffm. Common on the ground on grass-heaths, sand dunes, etc. Smaller than *P. canina*, often forming patches about 5cm across, with a glossy upper surface. It is greenish-brown when damp and greyish-brown when dry and the underside is white with brown veins, merging with a brown tomentum. Spore-producing discs are frequent (shown in photograph), reddish-brown discs, held erect and curved at the edges of lobes.

Parmelia caperata

Parmelia caperata (L.) Ach. Common in the south of England on old trees and sometimes rocks, rarer in the north. It is light yellowish-green and may form patches 6cm across with rounded lobes. The centre is usually wrinkled and covered with granular powdery yellowish-green vegetative reproduction structures (soredia). Spore-producing discs are rare (not shown in photograph) and are also formed in the centre and have dark reddish-brown discs.

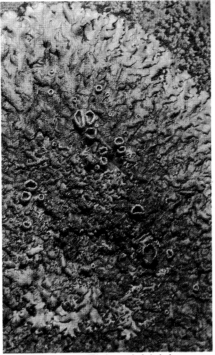

Parmelia conspersa (Ehrh. ex Ach.) Ach.
Common on siliceous rocks and walls in hilly
districts of Britain. It forms yellowish-grey
circular patches of flat lobes deeply divided
around the edge. Spore-producing discs are
dark brown or reddish-brown with elevated
yellowish-green margins. Rod-shaped
structures (isidia) are formed in the centre.

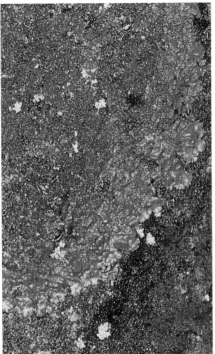

Parmelia glabratula (Lamy) Nyl. Common on
trees and occasionally on fences, forming
shiny, light brownish or olive leafy patches. It
is closely attached to its substrate and has
shallowly lobed edges. A continuous mass of
rod-like growths (isidia) is usually produced in
the centre and these are persistent.

Parmelia loxodes Nyl. Not uncommon on
siliceous rocks in the north and west, especially
near the sea. It forms greenish-brown patches
of rather crowded swollen lobes. They produce
clusters of rod-shaped growths on their surfaces
which often become eroded.

Parmelia mougeotii Schaerer. Common on
granite and schist boulders in the Scottish
highlands and scattered on suitable substrates
elsewhere. It forms round yellowish-grey
patches, up to about 3cm across with narrow
lobes at the margin. The centre is darker and
covered with scattered powdery vegetative
structures (soredia).

Parmelia omphalodes (L.) Ach. Common in
hilly and mountain districts on siliceous rocks
and walls forming loosely attached clumps of
brownish lobes, often with a metallic glint. The
surface has a fine network of pale lines and the
rod-shaped growths of other *Parmelia* species
are never formed. Spore-producing structures
are often found, reddish-brown discs with pale
margins.

Crottle *Parmelia saxatilis* (L.) Ach. Common
on trees, siliceous rocks and walls. Long used
as a wool-dye, producing a fast reddish-brown.
The thallus forms circular lobed patches, grey
when dry, greenish or bronzy when wet. The
surface is covered with a network of white or
grey lines. Mature plants have a mass of rod-
shaped projections (isidia) in the centre. Spore-
producing bodies are uncommon but are large
dark brown discs.

Parmelia subrudecta Nyl. Common in the south of Britain on trees, sometimes on rocks but rare in Scotland. It forms greenish-grey patches with rounded lobes which are light brown underneath. The round white, powdery clusters scattered over the surface are vegetative reproduction structures (soredia).

Parmelia subrudecta

Stereocaulon vesuvianum Pers. Common on mosses, siliceous rocks, walls or ground in upland areas, often in mineral-rich habitats. It consists of loosely branching stems clustered together forming a cushion. The stems are tough, light grey, about 1 to 5cm tall and covered with tiny rounded lobed scales.

Hypogymnia physodes (L.) Nyl., synonym *Parmelia physodes* (L.) Ach. Common throughout Britain on tree branches and twigs, wood, rocks, walls and soil, forming great masses or small patches of narrow smooth glaucous-grey lobes. The plant appears slightly inflated with a dark bare lower surface. Vegetative structures (soredia) are often produced at the ends of the lobes; these are white, powdery and lip-shaped.

Cladonia portentosa (Dufour) Zahlbr., synonym *C. impexa* Harm. Common on moors and heaths forming patches among heather stems and on bare ground. The many-branched stems are hollow and tips point in all directions, which distinguishes it from *C. arbuscula*. Spore-producing structures are uncommon but are brown and form at branch tips. Like *C. arbuscula*, this lichen contains usnic acid which imparts a yellowish tinge.

Hypogymnia physodes

Cladonia portentosa

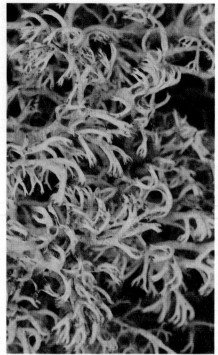

Cladonia arbuscula (Wallr.) Rabenh., synonym *C. sylvatica* auct. Common on mountains and hillsides, sandy or stony heaths, dunes and peat where it forms thick bushy yellow-tinged erect tufts. The stems are hollow and repeatedly branched with the coarse tips all bent in one direction. It contains an antibiotic, usnic acid, which imparts a yellowish coloration. Spores are produced in tiny brown structures at the tips of the branches.

Reindeer Moss *Cladonia rangiferina* (L.) Weber. Uncommon, found in the mountain regions of Scotland and Wales. In arctic and subarctic regions this is one of the most abundant plants and often forms a major component of the diet of reindeer and caribou. The whitish-grey plants may be up to about 8cm tall, with branches pointing in one direction. Spore-producing bodies are rare.

Cladonia uncialis (L.) Weber. Common on peaty moors. The thallus is formed into swollen yellowish-grey stems which are broad and hollow and forked several times into small pointed branches. At the points of branching there are clearly visible holes. The fruiting structures are formed at the tips of the branches, but are rare. It may attain a height of as much as 7cm in wet situations. The plant has a smooth surface.

Cladonia gracilis (L.) Willd. This lichen grows on both bare and peaty soils. The tall stems are greenish-brown or dark brown and are only slightly branched. They are smooth and some expand into narrow cups which carry the spore-producing bodies on their rims, whilst the majority have pointed tips. There are few scales at the base and no openings into the hollow stems are generally found.

Cladonia coniocraea (Flörke) Sprengel. Common on rotting wood, tree stumps and at the base of trees amongst mosses, more rarely on sandy or peaty soil. The hollow slender stalks arise from small greyish-green scales as in *C. fimbriata* but do not expand into cups. They are curved, taper to a point and are usually covered with grey-green powdery reproductive structures (soredia).

Cladonia squamosa (Scop.) Hoffm. Common on poor soil, stumps and rocks on moors, hillsides and woodlands. Patches of tiny greyish scales give rise to hollow straggly brownish-tinged stalks, sometimes forming a narrow cup and sometimes branched and tapered to pointed tips. Spore-producing structures are brown and produced at the apex. The outer layer peels away but remains attached, giving the plant the appearance of being covered with scales.

Cladonia fimbriata (L.) Fr. This lichen is common on walls, tree stumps and roots, dunes and banks in all but the wet mountain regions of Britain. Wide cups are borne on longer stalks than *C. pyxidata* and are coated with very fine grey-green powdery soredia. The stalks arise from a patch of tiny greyish scales which are white beneath. Spore-producing structures are dark brown and are produced on the rim of the cups.

Cladonia fimbriata

Cladonia subcervicornis (Vainio) Du Rietz. Usually seen as a mass of scales, elongated, about 0.75 to 2cm long, and divided into lobes, grey-green above and whitish below but blackened at the base. Common on blanket bog or among rocks, only in the west and north. Spore-producing structures are not common and are produced in clusters on smooth stalks.

Cup Lichen *Cladonia pyxidata* (L.) Hoffm. Common on banks, walls and rocks, often in dry places. It consists of grey or brown-grey scales with white under-surfaces. Broad warty granulose cups are produced from the basal scales; small brown spore-producing bodies are produced on the rims and no powdery bodies are formed.

Cup Lichen *Cladonia pyxidata*

Cladonia bellidiflora (Ach.) Schaerer. Common on mountain moorland in the Scottish highlands, rare elsewhere. Straggly yellowish-grey to greenish stalks, covered with scales, may reach about 5cm in height and are topped by clusters of large scarlet spore-producing structures. The stalks, called podetin, arise from patches of lobed scales on the ground.

Cladonia bellidiflora

Cladonia polydactyla (Flörke) Sprengel, synonym *C. flabelliformis* Vainio. Common on peaty or loamy soil on moorland and woodland or on tree bases and stumps, especially in the wet. Basal scales are small, blue-grey, deeply lobed and scattered; stalks are narrow and scaly at the base and slightly expanded at the tips into narrow cups which carry scarlet spore-producing bodies, and powdery vegetative structures (soredia).

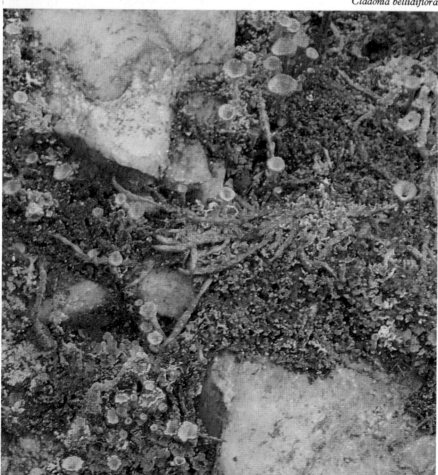

Cladonia coccifera (L.) Willd. Common on moors and hillsides especially at high altitudes. It forms patches of tiny scales, from which grow hollow warty stalks which are tinged yellow. These bear wide-mouthed cups which carry scarlet spore-producing structures on their rims.

Cladonia coccifera

Cladonia floerkeana (Fr.) Flörke. Common on peaty soil of moors and heaths. The basal scales form scattered patches. They are small and greenish-grey. Stalks are grey and simple or sparsely branched; scaly at the base and granular above. They do not form cups but bear large scarlet spore-producing bodies at the tips, thus resembling matchsticks.

Cladonia floerkeana

Lichina confinis (Müll.) Agardh. Common on rocks by the sea near the high-tide mark. It grows as blackish tufts of upright many-branched rounded stems, about 0.5cm tall. Spore-producing structures are formed in branch tips which become swollen.
L. pygmaea (Lightf.) Agardh is similar, but larger, to 1cm, with flattened lobes, except where round fruiting bodies are present. It grows lower down the shore.

Cetraria chlorophylla

Cetraria chlorophylla (Willd.) Vainio. Common in upland areas on fences and trees, especially conifers, and sometimes siliceous walls. It forms small deeply lobed, olive-green tufts, which are darker, brownish-green when dry, lighter in colour below. The lobed edges are very wavy and crisped and are covered with white, powdery reproductive structures. The photograph shows *Hypogymnia physodes* surrounding *C. chlorophylla*.

Platismatia glauca (L.) W.Culb & C. Culb.,
synonym *Cetraria glauca* (L.) Ach. Common
in hilly areas on trees and fences, walls and
rocks. Similar to *Cetraria chlorophylla*, but
when dry is usually blue-grey above and brown
to black below; when wet the upper surface is
blue-green. Spore-producing discs are rare and
white grainy vegetative structures are common
around the edges. The photograph also shows
Hypogymnia physodes.

Evernia prunastri (L.) Ach. Common on trees
and sometimes on fences, rocks, walls and soil.
It forms hanging tufts, 2 to 6cm long. The
forked branches are antler-shaped, greenish
grey on the upper surface and white below.
Powdery white soredia usually occur on the
margins of the lobes. Spore-producing
structures are pinkish or brown discs, and are
rare. This lichen is known as Mousse de
Chêne (Oak Moss) in France.

Pseudevernia furfuracea (L.) Zopf, synonyms
Parmelia furfuracea (L.) Ach., *Evernia
furfuracea* (L.) Mann. Most common in hilly
districts on trees, fences, rocks and walls. It is
light grey or white on its upper surface and
often black underneath. The upper surface is
often covered with granular projections. Spores
are rarely produced. *Hypogymnia physodes* is
also shown in the photograph.

Iceland Moss *Cetraria islandica* (L.) Ach.
Common in the north of England and Scotland
among heather on moors and mountains, rare
elsewhere. This lichen is edible and can be
made into a jelly after soaking in water to
remove its bitterness. The forked branches are
2 to 6cm tall, up to 1cm across and are edged
with a row of small spines. The plant is dark
chestnut brown on the upper surface and paler
beneath, and grows in erect tufts.

Thamnolia vermicularis (Swartz) Ach.
ex Schaerer. Common on mountain tops,
above 750m, in Scotland and Wales, often
growing among *Racomitrium* moss. It forms
pale grey hollow stems, resembling worms,
which produce neither spores nor soredia, but
spread when bits are broken off and fall in
suitable conditions for growth.

Roccella phycopsis (Ach.) Ach. Rare, found on
maritime rocks in parts of south-west England,
as far east as the Isle of Wight. Rounded pale
blue-grey tufts may be 5cm long and have
large whitish soredia on their surface. Black
spore-producing discs are not common.
R. fuciformis (L.) DC. is similar with longer,
more flattened branches. Once a source of
purple dye (but should not be collected as it is
now very rare).

Sphaerophorus globosus (Huds.) Vainio, synonym *S. coralloides* Pers. Common on mossy siliceous rocks, sometimes on tree trunks, in upland areas. It forms a much-branched brownish-grey coral-like tuft, about 1.5 to 5cm tall. Lower parts are stout and cylindrical, with smooth and brittle upper branches. The fruiting bodies are produced in globular structures at the shoot tips and burst open when ripe to expose a dark spore mass.

Cornicularia aculeata (Schreber) Ach. Common in dry places on heaths, dunes and moss-covered rocks, where it grows in tufts. The finely branched stems are dark shiny brown and quite prickly and wiry when dry. Wet specimens are paler, greenish and much softer. Each branch is flattened, about 0.1cm across and often edged with a row of bristles. Spore-producing structures are rare, small discs similar in colour to the rest of the plant.

Ramalina farinacea (L.) Ach. Common on tree trunks and twigs, rarely on rocks, forming thick tufts. The narrow branches are greenish-grey on both sides and on close examination the edges are seen to be covered with floury soredia in circular spots. Spores are produced in disc-like structures but these are very rare. Very stunted specimens occur in polluted areas.

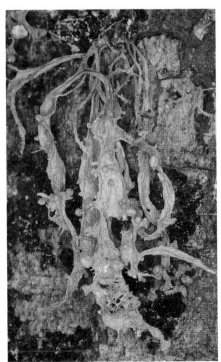

Ramalina fraxinea (L.) Ach. Common on trees, especially good specimens found in Scotland and in the West Country. It is often found on poplar trees in particular. It grows in tufts of broad branches 2 to 5cm long or more in favourable places. The surface is flat, sparsely branched, wrinkled and often broken. Spore-producing discs are common, on short stalks at the edges and on the surfaces of the branches.

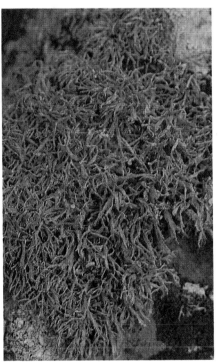

Sea Ivory *Ramalina siliquosa* (Huds.) A.L. Sm. Abundant on siliceous rocks near the sea above high-water mark. The yellowish-grey hanging or erect tufts are often flattened and strap-shaped with a smooth, hard and shiny surface, frequently warted. Spore-producing discs are common and are on very short stalks.

Ramalina subfarinacea (Nyl. ex Crombie) Nyl. Frequently found on siliceous rocks near the sea. The branched stems are yellowish-grey and grow in tufts. Circular floury reproductive structures (soredia) are produced on the branch edges.

Bryoria fuscescens

Bryoria fuscescens (Gyelnik.) Brodo. & D. Hawksw., synonym *Alectoria fuscescens* Gyelnik. Common on trees and fences in the mountain or hill districts of the north of Britain. It grows as tufts of hanging hair-like branches up to 15 or 20cm long, coloured pale or dark brown. They are much shorter in dry or polluted places. Fruiting structures are very rare, but small whitish vegetative structures are commonly found scattered on the stems.

Usnea subfloridana Stirt. Common on trees and sometimes on rocks, especially frequent in the hilly districts of the north of Britain. The grey-green much-branched tufts may be erect at first but soon become hanging, 3 to 8cm long from a blackish base. Small rod-shaped growths (isidia) are common.

Usnea florida (L.) Weber. Found on trees and fences, especially in the West Country, rare elsewhere. It forms stiff, more or less erect tufts with large cup-shaped spore-producing bodies (apothecia), which are more common than on other *Usnea* species. These are fringed by long thick hairs (cilia).

Usnea subfloridana

Usnea rubiginea (Michaux) Massal. Most frequent in Wales and south and west England, growing on tree trunks and branches. The tufts grow erect or hanging and are tinged reddish. They are usually covered with warts and rod-shaped growths (isidia) which become broken off with age.

Usnea rubiginea

Index of common names

*(*Denotes species not illustrated.)*

Index of botanical names

*(*Denotes species not illustrated. Synonyms are shown in italic.)*